D0915697

Tales from the 1969-1970
New York Knicks

Bill Gutman

www.SportsPublishingLLC.com

ISBN: 1-58261-808-9

Publishers: Peter L. Bannon and Joseph J. Bannon Sr.
Senior managing editor: Susan M. Moyer
Acquisitions editor: Noah Amstadter
Developmental editor: Regina D. Sabbia
Art director: K. Jeffrey Higgerson
Dust jacket design: Heidi Norsen
Interior layout and imaging: Greg Hickman and Kathryn R. Holleman
Photo editor: Erin Linden-Levy
Media and promotions managers: Kelley Brown (regional),
     Randy Fouts (national), Maurey Williamson (print)

Printed in the United States of America

Sports Publishing L.L.C.
804 North Neil Street
Champaign, IL 61820

Phone: 1-877-424-2665
Fax: 217-363-2073
www.SportsPublishingLLC.com

CONTENTS

INTRODUCTION

Before the 1969-1970 National Basketball season even began, the pressure was on the New York Knicks, and for a lot of reasons. For openers, one the NBA's so-called "flagship" franchises had never won a league championship going back to the initial season of 1946-1947. Add to that the fact that New York City had been a hotbed of basketball even before pro ball had become firmly established. The college game was always huge in the city, and its fans were among the most knowledgeable and supportive in the country. The city's main arena and the Knicks' home, Madison Square Garden, had been given the nickname "The Mecca of Basketball" long ago. In fact, when the new season opened, the Knicks would be playing in brand-new Madison Square Garden for just the second year, a modern arena with a capacity of nearly 20,000, one worthy of seeing an NBA championship flag hanging from the rafters.

There was still more. The New York Yankees and the NFL's New York Giants has been the town's big winners over the last couple of decades, especially after the Brooklyn Dodgers went west following the 1957 baseball season. But as of 1969, both the Yanks and Giants were in a down cycle, which ordinarily would make this sports-crazy town hungry for a winner. Then, in 1969, their appetites were satiated. In January, the New York Jets capped off the 1968 football season by becoming the first American Football League team to defeat an established NFL team in a title game that would soon become known as the Super Bowl. Led by quarterback Joe Namath, who was brazen enough to guarantee a victory, the Jets outplayed the heavily favored Colts and won it, 16-7, in a game still called one of the greatest upsets ever. So the Jets were champs in just their ninth year of existence, and the city went wild.

Then in October it happened again. Now it was the New York Mets' turn. The lowly Mets, brought to the National League and to New York in 1962—an expansion team given to the city to try to replace the departed Giants and Dodgers—had been league doormats every year, never finishing higher than ninth in a 10-team league. But in 1969, the Mets caught fire. Managed by former Dodger star Gil Hodges and led by a pair of outstanding young pitchers—Tom Seaver and Jerry Koosman—the Mets not only won 100 games in the regular season, but then swept the Atlanta Braves in the first ever divisional playoff series, and followed that by surprising the powerful and heavily favored Baltimore Orioles to win the World Series in five games. They had done it in just their eighth year of existence. Once again, the city of New York had a tickertape parade and another set of heroes.

That left the Knicks pretty much standing alone. Sure, the Rangers hadn't won a Stanley Cup since 1940, but at least they had given New York fans a taste of Stanley Cup champagne. The Knicks were oh-for-the-life-of-the-league, and that didn't sit well with the hoop crazed in the Big Apple. For nearly a decade and a half these perennially loyal Garden dwellers had sat hopelessly by as the Boston Celtics totally dominated the sport. Led by their great center, Bill Russell, and an outstanding cast of supporting characters, the Celtics had won 11 NBA titles in the past 13 years, leaving little room for anyone else. The only two teams to break the streak were the St. Louis Hawks in 1957-1958, when Russell was hurt, and the Philadelphia 76ers in 1966-1967, when Wilt Chamberlain showed he could be much more than a one-man wrecking crew. Otherwise, from 1956-1967 to 1968-1969 it was the Celtics, Celtics, Celtics, making perhaps the greatest sustained run of success in sports history.

Now, however, the door was open. Following the 1968-1969 season, in which the Celts rallied from a fourth-place regular-season finish to win yet another title, Bill Russell has retired. The dynasty was done, and pretty much everyone conceded that a new NBA champion would be crowned in 1969-1970. But would it be the Knicks? There were a number of factors that have been developing over the past several years that made fans think that the team had a chance.

Though the New Yorkers had made trips to the finals three straight years between 1950-1951 and 1952-1953, they came up short each time, losing to the Rochester Royals and then the Minneapolis Lakers twice. Just the geographical location of those two old franchises dates those early Knicks teams. After that it was always wait till next year. Between 1953-1954 and 1966-1967, the Knicks had just one winning season. And coming into the 1968-1969 season, they had finished with losing records for eight consecutive years. Not much to brag about for a team that played its games at the Mecca of Basketball. The team also had a reputation for making a series of poor draft picks and just not finding the right combination.

But by the middle of the 1968-1969 season, many felt the right combination was finally in place. Not only that. The Russell roadblock was also gone. And that's why, as the 1969-1970 season approached, optimism filled the air in and around Madison Square Garden. Could this be the year? Expectations were running high, and everyone knew it—the fans, the players, and their coach. For all those reasons, however, the pressure to win was also at an all-time high.

So let the games begin.

CHAPTER 1

SETTING THE STAGE ON THE GARDEN FLOOR AND AROUND THE LEAGUE

THE NBA WAS A LONG TIME COMING

It may come as a surprise to some basketball fans today, but the NBA is the baby among professional sports leagues. Baseball's National League was formed way back in 1876, joined by the American League in 1901. Two years later the World Series began. The National Hockey League began play in 1917, and it wasn't long before the Stanley Cup became the brass ring to which all teams aspired. In 1920, the National Football League came into existence, perhaps a far cry from what it is today, but it was the NFL nevertheless and has played continuously ever since. By that time basketball was already being played at many colleges, and there were professional teams, as well, but the rules were all over the place, and all early attempts to form one organized league ended in failure.

While Babe Ruth was hitting a ton of home runs and Red Grange was running wild on the gridiron, the world's greatest basketball players were barnstorming, going from game to game and playing for maybe $15 or $25 bucks a game. They often had to get to games by walking, by car, by ferry, or by train. They might find themselves playing on a court surrounded by a wire cage or a loose net. Or they might play in a basement with pillars to hold up the building right out on the *court*. They sometimes had to vacate the floor for halftime dances. Some baskets were attached to wire backboards, some to wood, while some had no backboard at all, just extended out on the court via a long pipe.

These early games were marked by some strange plays. When there was a net around the court a player could be trapped if he dribbled into the corner. The defender could grab the net on both sides and literally pull it around him. Held ball! In a game played with a cage around the court and no backboard, an early pro named Jack Inglis jumped up alongside the basket, grabbed the cage, and pulled himself up alongside the basket. While the defenders looked up at him helplessly, a teammate passed him the ball. Inglis caught it while hanging onto the cage with one hand and dropped it through the basket. An early version of the slam dunk. It was a perfectly legal play, because no one had ever seen it done before.

There were a few attempts at early leagues, but none of them lasted very long. Even in the 1930s, the professional leagues were usually played on the weekends, because the "pros" had to work at regular jobs during the week. They simply couldn't make enough money playing basketball to support themselves and their families. By the mid 1940s there were two professional leagues—the Basketball Association of America (BAA) and the National Basketball League (NBL). The BAA, the forerunner of the NBA, was played in the bigger cities and had the larger arenas, the while NBL had arguably the better teams and more of the top players, but the franchises were often located in small towns with the arenas not much more than small, drafty gyms. The beginning of the NBA is considered to be the 1946-1947 season when the league was still known as the Basketball

Association of America. Though no one could be sure at the time, professional basketball was finally here to stay. So even though the Knicks had never won an NBA title, the drought was only one of 23 years, nothing like the 86-year wait the Boston Red Sox had between their last World Series win in 1918 and their unexpected victory in 2004.

SOME STRANGE PLACES TO PLAY

Three of the top teams in the old NBL were the Minneapolis Lakers, Syracuse Nationals, and Rochester Royals. Along with the Fort Wayne Pistons, they would jump to the BAA in 1948-1949, increasing the league from eight to 12 teams. Other NBL teams would be taken in the following year when the final merger occurred, and the new, 17-team league was renamed the National Basketball Association. But while they were still part of the National Basketball League, the Lakers, Nationals, and Royals played in some of those small arenas that just wouldn't work as the league grew. That's why the franchises were eventually relocated. The Royals, for instance, played in a bandbox called the Edgerton Park Arena in Rochester that was so pressed for space that the backboards were attached directly to the walls at both ends. That gave players driving to the hoop just three choices. They could either try to stop on a dime, run into the wall, or run through the doors at the ends of the arena. During the winter months, someone was stationed at both doors and would open them quickly when a player came toward them at full speed.

This wasn't always the best idea. Players might not hit the wall if they chose to run out into the night air, but there were hazards involved in that choice, as well. Sometimes a player would collide with late-arriving spectators. Other times, when there were heavy snowfalls, he might make it through the doors only to be stopped by a snowbank outside. More than once, a player who drove to the hoop for a layup and then ran through the open door, would return to play with snow covering his sneakers and legs.

In Syracuse, the fans always hated Minneapolis center George Mikan. The 6'10" Mikan was basketball's first great big man, and because of him, the Lakers became a league powerhouse. Then one day Mikan made the mistake of complaining about the cigar smoke inside the Syracuse arena. That was all the fans had to hear. The next time the Lakers came to town the fans were ready. Almost everyone lit up as soon as the game began and the arena was soon enveloped by a smoky haze that must have made it look like a London fog. That's surely something that couldn't happen in the smoking-restricted world of today.

WHAT'S A TRI-CITIES?

Among the former NBL teams to join the new NBA in 1949-1950 were a number of franchises located in small cities throughout the Midwest. Some say the league took them in simply to avoid the possibility of anti-trust suits. At any rate, the new NBA was now comprised of three divisions and 17 teams, adding tiny franchises such as the Anderson Packers, Sheboygan Redskins, and Waterloo Hawks, as well as perhaps the strangest of all, a franchise called Tri-Cities. By 1954, the league was back to eight teams in two divisions and stayed that way through 1960. Definitely there were growing pains, and the small just did not survive.

But getting back to Tri-Cities. In 1949-1950, Holy Cross in Massachusetts had an All-America guard named Bob Cousy. When the NBA draft rolled around, Cooz learned he had been drafted by the only franchise that didn't have a city for name.

Totally confused, he asked a now famous question: "What's a tri-cities?"

The answer was that the franchise was actually located in Moline, Illinois, but divided its home games between Moline and two other small Illinois cities. Thus, Tri-Cities. Fortunately, Cousy never had to experience that kind of nomadic home schedule firsthand. Before the season began he was traded to the Chicago Stags, and when the Stags folded, the players were divided up among the surviving teams. When there were just three players left—Cousy included—the names were placed in a hat, and the Knicks, Philadelphia Warriors, and Celtics lined up to take their pick. The Knicks drew first and were overjoyed to pick all-star Max Zaslofsky. Next came the Warriors, and they drew the name of veteran guard Andy Phillip. No complaints in Philly. But Boston wasn't happy. Red Auerbach's Celtics were left with the rookie Cousy.

As it turned out, Cousy went on to become the greatest guard of his time, a magician with the ball who triggered the unstoppable Celtic fast break. His name is now synonymous with Boston and basketball immortality. Had the Knicks drawn his name, the whole history of the franchise might have been changed. As for Cooz, he might not have known what a Tri-Cities was, but he sure knew what to do with the basketball once he had it in his large hands.

Just for the record, Tri-Cities survived. In 1951 the franchise moved to Milwaukee. Later, the Milwaukee Hawks became the St. Louis Hawks and eventually today's Atlanta Hawks. It was a long journey that began when one of the greatest players in NBA history couldn't figure out what a Tri-Cities was.

THE CELTICS DOMINATE

Despite the presence of Cousy and fellow guard Bill Sharman, the Celtics were a good, but not great team in the 1955-1956 season. They finished six games behind the Philadelphia Warriors in the NBA Eastern Division and four games ahead of the 35-37 Knicks. The Warriors would win the NBA crown that year, but things were about to change. That same season, college basketball was being dominated by the University of San Francisco, which had won its second consecutive NCAA championship and with a win streak that had gone past 50 games. The team had a great guard in K.C. Jones, and several other fine players, but the secret ingredient was their 6'9" center, Bill Russell. Not only could Russell score, but he was a tenacious defender and rebounder. His presence in the middle was the reason the college rules committee expanded the free throw lane from six feet to 12 feet between his junior and senior years.

"We weren't planning to make any changes in the foul lane," said Al "Doggie" Julian of Dartmouth, "but after some of the coaches saw Russell's performance they got scared and pushed through the 12-foot lane."

The rule was designed to keep Russell farther from the basket, figuring he wouldn't be able to block or alter as many shots, nor tap in as many of his teammates' misses. But because of his speed, Russell was just as effective with the wider lane and was fully used to it when he joined the NBA. Though Russell had announced that he would represent the United States in the Olympic Games at Melbourne, causing him to miss the first two months of the NBA season, Boston's Red Auerbach wanted him badly. He traded up to the two-spot in the draft by giving the St. Louis Hawks all-star forward "Easy" Ed Macauley and former St.

Louis University star Cliff Hagan for the rights to draft Russell. Auerbach got his man and changed the face of the NBA forever.

Russell was everything expected and more. In addition to his great defensive and rebounding prowess, he had an unquenchable thirst to win. He was so tight before every game he played that he would invariably throw up before taking the court. And God forbid if the Celtics lost. Neither Russell nor team leader Cousy ever wanted to lose two straight. Most times they were even better after a loss, if that was possible. With Russell averaging a record 19.6 rebounds in 48 games, the Celtics stormed to the front of the Eastern Division and won their first NBA title by beating the Hawks in seven games. It was the beginning of their record run of 11 titles in 13 seasons.

Anything Russell gave the Celts on offense was a bonus. It was his defensive prowess that changed the game. Most centers before him, even the great Mikan, were big but immobile. Russell was not only fast, but had an uncanny sense of timing. He blocked shots like no one before him, grabbed rebounds, and his quick outlet passes started a fast break that often caught opponents sitting on their heels. With Cousy's ballhandling prowess and wizard-like passing, the Celtics' fast break became an unstoppable weapon. Even as the supporting cast changed over the years, Russell continued as the anchor that kept Boston as the NBA's best right through 1968-1969.

A STAR-STUDDED NBA IN THE 1960S

In 1960, the United States assembled a team of amateur basketball players to represent their country at the Olympic Games in Rome. That was long before the day when NBA players, professionals, could also be Olympic athletes. These were mostly college players about to go to the NBA. Among the players on that undefeated, gold medal-winning team were Oscar

Robertson, Jerry West, Jerry Lucas, Walt Bellamy, Terry Dischinger, Darrell Imhoff, and Adrian Smith. All of them would go on to outstanding NBA careers beginning that fall, with Robertson, West, and Lucas among the all-time greats.

They were part of a change that was coming over the league, then in just its 15th season. If Russell was emblematic of the new breed of big man, Wilt Chamberlain represented an even bigger version of a dominant center. Wilt joined the league in 1959-1960, setting up a decade-long duel with Russell that is still talked about today. The Lakers' Elgin Baylor was a 6'5" forward who could handle the ball like a guard and seemed to hang in the air just a fraction longer than his defender when he went up for his shot. Big Bob Pettit was a virtual scoring machine, while Philly's Guy Rodgers did many of the same things in the backcourt that Cousy could do.

Then the class of 1960-1961, led by Robertson and West, arrived and were soon followed over the next few years by Bellamy, Lucas, center Nate Thurmond, swingman John Havlicek, guards Hal Greer and Lenny Wilkens, forwards Chet Walker and Gus Johnson, among others. And they would continue to come during the remainder of the decade, great ballplayers who played the game at a level well above most of their counterparts from the 1950s. The game and the players were getting better, and that's why the fans of the New York Knickerbockers were becoming antsy. None of these great stars managed to find their way to Madison Square Garden, unless they were wearing the uniform of the visiting team.

In 1963-1964, for example, the roster of the league's top scorers read Chamberlain, Robertson, Pettit, Bellamy, West, Baylor. Read the stats on the best rebounders, and you had Russell, Chamberlain, Lucas, Bellamy, Pettit. The top guys in assists were Robertson, Rodgers, K.C. Jones, West, Chamberlain. Not a single New York Knicks player among them. Why was it that the Knicks, with their perennial losing record, couldn't seem to land a superstar, a player to lead the resurgence that the fans kept hoping for, year after year?

At the end of the 1963-1964 season, the Knicks roster read like a list of has-beens, never-weres, and never-would-bes. Len Chappell, Bob Boozer, John Green, Art Heyman, Bill McGill, John Egan, Tom Gola, Al Butler, John Rudometkin, Dave Budd, Tom Hoover, and Gene Conley. This group, along with a few others who departed during the year, could do no better than 22-58, the poorest record in the entire league. With this club, thoughts of a league title must have seemed like a fairy tale, at best, something that could only happen in the far reaches of never-never land.

THE WORLD'S MOST FAMOUS ARENA

It would be hard to find a real sports fan anywhere who hasn't heard of Madison Square Garden. For years, the Garden has been the focal point of basketball in New York. A newspaperman named Ned Irish was the first to see the potential of putting college basketball into the Garden. In the early and mid-1930s, Irish saw the money-making potential of the sport as well as the value of scheduling popular New York teams into the Garden for big games, taking them out of small gymnasiums that might only hold 1,000 or 2,000 spectators. Soon, nearly 16,000 fans were jamming the Garden to see their local favorites as well as major college teams from out of state.

The first doubleheader was held on December 29, 1934, with St. John's playing Westminster College of Pennsylvania, then a basketball power, followed by New York University going up against Notre Dame. Irish was hoping for a crowd of 10,000 fans, saying, "Metropolitan college basketball will step out of its cramped gymnasiums and gloomy armories tonight and into the bright lights and spaciousness of Madison Square Garden for the first of a series of six doubleheaders arranged in the hope of proving this winter that the sport deserves and will thrive in a major league setting."

Irish's optimism was more than fully rewarded when 16,138 fans jammed the Garden for that first doubleheader. From that point on, New York and basketball became big-time partners. There was a downside to all this, as well. Big-time partners also led to partners in crime. The large crowds and excitement over the games also led to increased betting, and the gamblers were soon in abundance among the throngs. That led to several college basketball scandals over the ensuing decades that involved numerous college athletes, but didn't dim the enthusiasm for having basketball shows at the Garden.

There have actually been four different Madison Square Gardens. The first opened way back in 1879 at Fifth Avenue and 23rd Street. It was originally an abandoned railroad shed converted into a sports arena and described in *Harper Weekly* magazine as "grimy, drafty, and combustible." Then in 1890, the Garden underwent a $3 million renovation on the same site with the new structure designed by architect Stanford White. White was as well known for his womanizing as for his talent as an architect, and in 1906 he was shot to death in the Garden's rooftop restaurant by the jealous husband of an ex-girlfriend. It was one of New York's most infamous early scandals.

Finally, in December of 1925, a new Madison Square Garden arose at Eighth Avenue and 50th Street, the structure that began housing those doubleheaders in the 1930s. The building was also used for ice hockey, boxing matches, the Ringling Brothers Barnam & Bailey Circus, political conventions, and a variety of other events. When the Knicks first began playing there, pro basketball didn't rank very high up the ladder of important events, and the team was often usurped by the circus and other shows, sending the Knicks to the much smaller 69th Street Regiment Armory.

In 1968, the present day Garden opened 17 blocks south, on Seventh Avenue and 33rd Street, above Pennsylvania Station. The timing couldn't have been better. The new structure, which housed 19,500 fans for basketball and 18,200 for hockey, opened on February 14, 1968, just as the Knicks were becoming an NBA force that would not be bumped to an armory because of the circus or anything else. Its debut brought the Garden into the modern world.

The former Garden, the one at Eighth Avenue and 50th, was built up rather than out. It was a slightly more intimate setting than the present-day garden, but the seats weren't as comfortable, and the view wasn't always perfect. If you were watching a hockey game from the mezzanine section, you couldn't see the near boards. Fans often stood the entire game and leaned as far forward as they could in order to see the action below them. The stairwells were very narrow, making it difficult and often time-consuming to leave the building. Like many other older arenas, the ventilation system wasn't very efficient, and by the second half of a game there would be a cloud of cigar and cigarette smoke gathered near the rafters and working its way down toward the floor. But because of the great events that came there, the fans didn't care. It was their place and they loved it.

Today's Madison Square Garden has unobstructed views of the court and the ice, though its wider construction puts some fans farther from the action. No matter, it is a modern arena with comfortable seating and all the amenities needed to enjoy a sporting event. It is still known as the world's greatest arena and the Mecca of basketball, but when it opened in the winter of 1968 no one could have known that within a year from its debut, the new Madison Square Garden would also house the best basketball team in the world.

CHAPTER 2

BEGINNING TO PUT THE PIECES IN PLACE

WINNING A LOST COMMODITY

New York has always loved a winner, maybe more so than other sports-crazed cities. If you win in the Big Apple, the fans will embrace you. If not...well, expect the boos, catcalls, and criticisms from everywhere. The City has always had a reputation for having some of the most knowledgeable fans in the world. They can see through the excuses and phonies, and they know the real goods from the cheap imitations. That said, New York fans have also proved incredibly patient. Last year's disappointment quickly becomes this year's optimism. Hope always springs eternal until another team falls on its face. That's how it was with the Knicks, especially from the mid-1950s to the early 1960s. The byword was losing, and fans at Madison Square Garden witnessed one sub-.500 team after another.

From 1954 to 1963, the following players were introduced to New York Knicks fans as the team's number-one draft choice. Jack Turner, Ken Sears, Ronnie Shavlik, Brendan McCann, Pete

Brannan, Johnny Green, Darrall Imhoff, Tom Stith, Paul Hogue, and Art Heyman. Some were All-Americans and outstanding collegiate players, but once they came to the Knicks they all took the low road. None of them surprised in a pleasant way. And during this time, the team was also playing the game of musical coaches. Joe Lapchick, who had coached the Knicks successfully since 1947-1948, left toward the end of the 1955-1956 season. Over the next decade through 1965-1966, the revolving door of coaches included Vince Boryla, Fuzzy Levane, Carl Braun, Eddie Donovan, Harry Gallatin, and Dick McGuire. Counting Lapchick, that's seven coaches in 10 years. It's not easy to build a winner with constant change at the top, not to mention an always unstable roster.

The team was especially futile during the early and middle years of the 1960s, when that large group of great players began coming into the NBA but somehow avoided landing with the Knicks. From 1959-1960 through 1965-1966 the team finished with marks of 27-48, 21-58, 29-51, 21-59, 22-58, 31-49, and 30-50. So there were very few Garden parties at the Mecca of basketball. With that kind of futility at the time when the game had become more exciting than ever, it's no wonder that the fans in New York hungered for a winner but always came away with their stomachs empty. With the new Garden opening in 1968, the timing couldn't have been better.

WILT'S BIG NIGHT AGAINST...WHO ELSE?

Perhaps the event most symbolic of the Knicks' futility during this period occurred on the night of March 2, 1962. It would be a night that the Knicks had their shooting eyes, would score 147 points...and still lose. Their opponent that night was the Philadelphia Warriors and their 7'1", 275-pound center, Wilt Chamberlain. Already the greatest offensive force the game had ever known, Wilt was on his way to averaging an incredible 50.4 points a game that season. The only defensive player who could put up any kind of battle against Wilt was Bill Russell. But on this night against the undermanned Knicks, Wilt even outdid himself.

The NBA game had still not completely escaped the shadows of being a minor league sport in 1961-1962, and this contest was played on what was called a neutral court in Hershey, Pennsylvania, not exactly a booming metropolis. But the NBA often scheduled these out-of-the-way games back then, and because of that there is no filmed record of this incredible night. Wilt went to work early, scoring on a variety of dunks, finger-rolls, and fadeaway jumpers—his usual itinerary—and was credited with 13 of his team's first 19 points. At the end of the first quarter the Warriors had a 42-26 lead with Wilt scoring 23. Most players would be satisfied with that as a helluva night's work. But the big guy was just tuning up at the expense of the lowly Knicks.

Wilt continued to shoot and score in the run-and-gun game that saw both clubs getting off shots long before the 24-second clock expired. At the half, it was still something of a ballgame. Philly had just a 79-68 lead, with Wilt canning 41 of his team's points. Earlier that season in December, the big guy had set a new single-game scoring mark with 78 points in a triple-overtime contest against the Lakers. Then in January, he broke the great Elgin Baylor's record of 71 in regulation by scoring 73 in a game at Chicago. Now he seemed poised to once again blow all the old records away. By the end of the third quarter Chamberlain had 69 as the Knicks defenders looked up helplessly while they watched him work his scoring magic. Now, it just seemed a matter of how high he could go.

With 10:10 left in the game, Wilt scored his 75th point, another new record in regulation, and by this time his teammates were feeding him the ball with a purpose. The points continued to come. Just before the five-minute mark, Wilt took an alley-oop pass from Al Attles and slammed home his 89th point as the Knicks tried valiantly to stop him. As the time continued to tick down, the big guy went over 90, then 92, 94, and finally 96 on a fadeaway jumper. Another dunk gave him 98 points with 1:19 left. Could he get the two more he needed to reach 100, something that seemed virtually impossible? He missed his next attempt and then, with the clock running down, Wilt went high in the air to grab a lob from Joe Ruklick and slammed it home for his 100th point of the game.

Philly won the game, 169-147. Wilt had hit on 36 of his 63 field goal tries and added an amazing 28 of 32 from the foul line, maybe his best night ever from the charity stripe. Amazingly, the Knicks had three players over the 30-point mark. Guard Richie Guerin, a fine player and scorer, had 39, Cleveland Buckner scored 33, and Willie Naulls chipped in 31. Ordinarily, having three players score 103 points between them would be enough to win most games. But this wasn't most games. It was a night when Wilt Chamberlain played like Superman, scoring an amazing 100 points, once again making Knicks fans wonder just when their team would stop being a doormat for the rest of the basketball world.

A DRAFT THAT DIDN'T CAUSE A COLD

Eddie Donovan had just completed his third full year as the Knicks coach at the end of 1963-1964. His teams had won only 43 games over the last two seasons, and Donovan was worried about his job. Duke All-American Art Heyman had been the team's number-one draft pick a year earlier, and while he averaged more than 15 points a game as a rookie, it was already obvious that he wasn't a long-term answer. With the 1964 draft approaching, the Knicks looked to end years of rookie futility. Then they made their picks.

In the first round they chose Jim "Bad News" Barnes, a 6'8" All-America forward from Texas Western, a guy who could both score and rebound. The "Bad News" supposedly referred to what Barnes brought to his opponents, but Knicks fans couldn't help hoping it didn't describe the draft choice himself. Then came the second round. That's when the Knicks surprised a lot of people by tabbing 6'9" center Willis Reed out of Grambling, making him the 10th player chosen. Playing at Grambling, an NAIA school in Louisiana, Reed didn't have the big reputation. The stats said that he led his school to three Southwestern Athletic Conference Championships and one NAIA crown, and that he had averaged 26.6 points and 21.3 rebounds as a senior, but no one in New York had the foggiest idea whether he could compete with the Russells and Chamberlains of the NBA and be the big man the Knicks had always needed. So the jury was still out.

The team also made some noise with their third pick, point guard Howard "Butch" Komives out of Bowling Green. They weren't getting the Big O or Jerry West, but Komives was a combative sort and just might have the ability to run things in the backcourt. Hey, three draft picks who looked as if they could contribute, maybe contribute big time. Though no one was ready to bet the farm, maybe, just maybe, the Knicks had hit pay dirt this time.

CLOSER, BUT NOT QUITE THE CIGAR

With their three rookies in the lineup the Knicks were a better team in 1964-1965, but still not a good one. They would finish at 31-49, last in the Eastern Division. In fact, in the entire NBA, only the Western Division San Francisco Warriors had a worse mark. But optimists pointed to the nine-game improvement over the season before as well as to the young players, though in reality, only one of them looked to be the real deal.

Jim Barnes had some good nights, but was inconsistent and left questions about his ability to bang against the top forwards in the league. He was the team's second leading scorer (15.5) and rebounder (9.7), but those with a discerning eye for talent had their doubts that he would mature into a real force. The Knicks would trade him to Baltimore the following year where he would pretty much duplicate his rookie numbers, then would fade after that.

Komives, also a second-round pick with Reed, wasn't a bad little player. He averaged 12.2 points his rookie year and led the team in assists, though his total of 265 didn't put him up among the league leaders. He would stay with the club until the huge trade in 1968-1969 that brought Dave DeBusschere to the team. But all too often, Komives didn't get along with his teammates and, as his assists totals prove, wasn't the kind of player who made those around him better. But as of 1964-1965, he did represent an upgrade.

The third rookie, Willis Reed, was another story. At 6'9", 240 pounds, Reed certainly wasn't among the tallest centers in the league. On the contrary, standing alongside a Wilt Chamberlain and later a Lew Alcindor (aka Kareem Abdul-Jabbar), he looked more like a forward than a center. Reed also wasn't the fastest big man in the league, lacking the speed and quick reactions of a Bill Russell. But he had other qualities that came to the fore almost immediately. Willis Reed could play against anyone because of his strength, toughness, heart, and will to excel and win. He was fundamentally sound, had a fine left-handed jump shot that he could take outside, and his strength and toughness allowed him to get underneath and rebound with the best of them. From the outset, he was up among both the scoring and rebounding leaders and had established himself as the leader of the new Knicks.

In a March game against the L.A. Lakers, Reed was on fire from the start. Hitting on a variety of jumpers and short hooks inside he torched the Lakers for 46 points, second highest total ever for a Knicks rookie. By the time the season ended, Reed has established himself. He was seventh in league in scoring (19.5 ppg) and fifth in rebounding (14.5 rpg). The only players ahead of him in scoring were Chamberlain, West, Robertson, Sam Jones of Boston, Baylor, and Walt Bellamy of Baltimore. The quartet of players getting more rebounds was Russell, Chamberlain, Nate Thurmond of San Francisco, and Jerry Lucas of Cincinnati. So Reed was right up there with the top Who's Who players in the game. Maybe, at long last, the team had itself a coming star.

THE FACE OF THE TEAM CHANGES, AND SO DOES THE CHEMISTRY

Still looking for the right combination, the Knicks made another move shortly after the start of the 1965-1966 season. When it was first announced, it had the New York fans' juices flowing. The Knicks announced they were sending Jim Barnes, their former top draft choice from a year earlier, along with a pair of veterans, forward Johnny Green and guard Johnny Egan, to the Baltimore Bullets in return for 6'11" center Walt Bellamy. The reason the fans were juiced? They saw Bellamy and San Francisco's Nate Thurmond as possibly the only two centers in the NBA who could play Wilt and Russell on almost even terms. Now Big Bells was coming to New York.

After a stellar career at the University of Indiana, where he averaged 20.6 points and 15.5 rebounds, Bellamy joined the expansionist Chicago Packers for the 1961-1962 season. All he did was average 31.6 points a game, second in the league to Wilt's record 50.4, and grab 1,500 rebounds, an average of 19 caroms a game, and behind only perennial leaders Chamberlain and Russell. In the eyes of many, Big Bells was about to become the NBA's third super center. But it never quite happened. The Packers changed their name to the Zephyrs a season later, then in 1963-1964 moved to Baltimore and became the Bullets. During this time Bellamy's numbers, while still good, began slipping.

By 1964-1965 he was averaging 24.8 points and 14.6 rebounds, still formidable, but not up to the standard he set as a rookie three years earlier. Bellamy almost never missed a game, at least physically. What people were beginning to realize is that the same Big Bells didn't show up every night. When he was going up against a Russell, Chamberlain, or Thurmond, he could be magnificent, showing talent at both ends of the court nearly equal to that of the man he was playing. But when the opponent was a Reggie Harding, a Darrall Imhoff, or any center of lesser talent, Bellamy often went to sleep. In other words, he played to the quality of the opposition.

But the Knicks still wanted him, their thinking being that with Bellamy at center and Reed moving to power forward, they would have a front line that could stand up to the rest of the league. There were two problems with that thinking. One was that Reed didn't like the move. "I'm a natural center," he said, referring to the position he had played all his life. And secondly, the Knicks learned quickly what others had known for a few years. You could never be sure just what Walt Bellamy would give you and when he would decide to give his best.

With Bellamy in the line up for the final 72 games of the season, the Knicks were still last with a 30-50 record, actually one game poorer than the season before. Bellamy averaged 23.2 points to lead the Knicks, followed by 23.1 points from guard Dick Barnett, who had come over in a trade with L.A. before the season. Reed's numbers suffered at power forward. He averaged just 15.5 points and 11.6 rebounds, and was obviously not as effective at power forward as he had been at center. It appeared once again that management had mismanaged Bellamy. The player who was viewed as a possible savior and superstar was not only disappointing, but his presence skewed the chemistry of the ballclub. Willis Reed simply wasn't a power forward. He was a center, but two guys couldn't play that position at the same time.

Same old Knicks thought many of their loyal but tiring fans.

A DRAFT-DAY GAMBLE

Even before the trade that brought Walt Bellamy to the team, the Knicks made another move that had their fans asking questions. The team had two first-round draft picks in 1965, and with one of them tabbed Dave Stallworth, a 6'7" forward from Wichita State. Dave "The Rave" was a flashy player who could score but wasn't exactly a "can't-miss" type. It was the second choice that left people wondering, not because of the talent of the player involved, but rather because no one knew for sure if he'd ever want to play in the NBA.

His name was Bill Bradley, and he had single-handedly put Princeton basketball on the map. No one spoke of scholarly Princeton in the same breath as UCLA, Duke, or Indiana when it came to prowess on the hardwood, but Bradley had changed all that. At 6'5", 200 pounds, he was far from an imposing physical presence. But after scoring 3.068 points for Crystal City High in Crystal City, Missouri, Bradley was on the basketball map. He had more than 70 scholarship offers, including one from the legendary Adolph Rupp at Kentucky, but the cerebral Bradley wanted no part of the Baron and the basketball factory he ran at Lexington. His life was much broader than the dimensions of a basketball court, and thus he opted to matriculate at Princeton.

The Knicks were gambling on the future when they drafted Oxford-bound Bill Bradley in 1965. Bradley returned to play for the Knicks two years later and became an integral part of the team. AP/WWP

Bradley entered Princeton in the fall of 1961 and immediately began making his mark both on the basketball court and in the classroom. As a sophomore, Bradley would average 27.3 points and 12.2 rebounds a game, but he would really attract national attention as a senior at Madison Square Garden's Holiday Festival in December of 1964. Princeton went up against a top-rated and powerful Michigan team, led by All-American Cazzie Russell, and Bradley was simply incredible. His shots seemed to have radar. He moved about the court effortlessly and constantly, getting open for a variety of jumpers and drives. With the huge crowd at the Garden cheering his almost unbelievable performance, he had the Tigers in front almost all the way. Then, after scoring 41 points and his team leading, 75-63, Bradley fouled out. In the few minutes remaining, Michigan rallied against the Bradley-less Princeton to win the game, 80-78. But Bradley had put on an unforgettable performance, yet he never forgot the effect of his fouling out.

"You can imagine how frustrated I felt," he said, "after scoring 41 points, to sit on the bench and watch the lead dissipate. Michigan closed the game with a 17-1 run, with Russell scoring nine of their 17 points, securing the Wolverines' 80-78 victory."

By that time, however, Bill Bradley was being called the best in the country by many. He reinforced that image in the NCAA tournament that year, leading Princeton into the final four, and then scoring 58 points against Wichita State in the Consolation Game for third place.

Bradley became a two-time consensus All-American, named Player of the Year in 1965 by the AP, UPI, and USBWA, and he averaged an amazing 30.2 points a game for his collegiate career. He was projected as a definite top choice in the NBA draft...except for one thing. Not surprisingly, Bill Bradley was also an Academic All-American, and it was already announced that he had been offered a prestigious Rhodes scholarship to study at Oxford University in England for two years. Before the NBA draft was even held, Bradley announced he would forsake professional basketball to study at Oxford. So when the Knicks tabbed him in the first round of the 1965 draft, they were betting on the future, betting that they could convince Bradley to return to the NBA in 1967 when his days at Oxford were over. It was a calculated gamble, the kind the Knicks always seemed to lose.

BETTER, BUT ONLY BY INCHES

Once again, in 1966, the Knicks had the first pick in the draft. This time it appeared they couldn't miss. They took Michigan All-American Cazzie Russell, a 6'5", 220-pound forward who had led the Wolverines to three Big Ten titles and a guy who averaged 27.1 points during his three-year collegiate career, including a school single-season mark of 30.1 points. Russell was a physical specimen who certainly appeared more than fully capable of handling the rough play in the NBA. Fans envisioned him stepping in and giving the team a 20-point scorer right from the start.

Though Cazzie showed flashes of his college skills, he proved to be another rookie who had to find his way. He averaged just 11.3 points a game, while Willis Reed, still playing at power forward, re-emerged as the team's star. Willis averaged 20.9 points, eighth best in the league, and 14.6 rebounds (sixth best) as the team inched forward to 36-45 finish, putting them in fourth place. Walt Bellamy's numbers, however, continued to drop. Big Bells averaged 19.0 points and 13.5 rebounds, a far cry from the 31.6 and 19.0 of his rookie season when he was looked upon as the third coming of Russell and Chamberlain. By now fans were getting used to the vagaries that characterized Bellamy's play. On some nights he was great; on others he was little more than ordinary. His inconsistency was beginning to wear on the Madison Square Garden faithful.

The Knicks had been a solid home team in 1966-1967, running up a 20-15 mark at the Garden. On the road, however, they were horrid, checking in at 9-24. Playing on the anachronistic neutral courts, they were 7-6. The team showed it could score points. Besides Reed and Bellamy, who were 1-2, they had Dick Barnett at 17.0, Howard Komives at 15.7, second-year guard/forward Dick Van Arsdale at 15.1, Dave Stallworth at 13.0, and the aforementioned Russell at 11.3. So they could put the ball in the hoop. With a couple of horses like Reed and Bellamy working close to the basket, you would think the team would also excel defensively. But they didn't, allowing three more points per game than they scored. Defense, or the lack thereof, seemed to be the main reason the team couldn't move further up the ladder.

If they were going to win, they would still have to revise the basic formula. It simply wasn't working.

THE TRANSITION BEGINS

If you're going to talk about the 1969-1970 Knicks, you have to begin with 1967-1968. That was the year the pieces began to fall into place. For openers, the Knicks' top draft choice that year was a 6'4" guard out of Southern Illinois named Walt Frazier. Knicks fans might have asked "Walt Who?" and booed the selection loudly had they not seen the slick guard lead the Salukis to the National Invitation Tournament championship a few months earlier. Southern Illinois was the first so-called small school to win the NIT, and Frazier played as if he had ice water in his veins. Maybe, just maybe, the always-critical and sometimes cynical fans felt, this guy can play.

That wasn't the only story. Generating even more excitement was the news out of England. Bill Bradley was completing his two-year course of studies at Oxford and had decided to play professional basketball after all. Bradley would say later that when he flew off to Oxford he never expected to return to the hardwood. Then, one day, he found a hoop and began shooting—by himself and with no one around—and it dawned on him that there would always be a great void in his life if he didn't return and test himself against the best players in the world. He had signed a $500,000, four-year contract with the Knicks, earning him the nickname "Dollar Bill." But the money notwithstanding, Bradley would be joining the Knicks for the 1967-1968 season. While at Princeton, Bradley had been all-everything, an absolute wonder on the court. But some couldn't help thinking now just how the two-year layoff would affect Bradley's consummate court skills. And, at 6'5", he was another of those mysterious swingmen. Would he be better at guard or forward? Or would he forever be caught in between?

The fans were already beginning to think that about Cazzie Russell. As a rookie, Cazzie played a lot of guard and was often exposed as being too slow for the position, on both offense and defense. Now they were getting a player of similar size, less strength, and a guy who had been away for two years. But, hey, he was still Bill Bradley. Wouldn't it be great if both Bradley and Russell could regain the magic they had at that memorable Holiday Festival meet at the Garden three years before? One could wish, if nothing else.

ANOTHER SLOW START

At the beginning of the 1967-1968 season it looked like more of the same. Bellamy continued to produce his on-again, off-again performances at center. Reed was playing well, but still

Lanky forward Phil Jackson fit into Coach Holzman's defensive scheme, but he missed the 1969-1970 season due to back surgery. Jackson would go on to become one of the most successful coaches in NBA history.
Photo by Vernon J. Biever

didn't look completely comfortable or happy at power forward. Russell, now at small forward, was scoring better, but still not playing like the superstar the Knicks envisioned when they drafted him. The veteran Barnett was consistent as always, and the rookie Frazier was sharing time with Howard Komives at point guard.

From the start, it was obvious that Bradley wasn't going to step in where he left off. There was plenty of rust around the edges. Dollar Bill would have to be worked into the rotation slowly. Dick Van Arsdale, rookie forward Phil Jackson, and guard Emmett Bryant were all contributing, but the team had suffered a loss when Dave Stallworth was diagnosed as having had a minor heart attack at a very early age. He wouldn't play a game all year.

This combo got off to a 15-22 start under coach Dick McGuire. McGuire, a former Knicks guard from earlier times, had continued the coaching merry-go-round that had characterized the team over the past decade. He had taken over for another former Knick, Harry Gallatin, who coached from mid-1964-1965 to early the following year. McGuire had finished off that year for Gallatin, coached the entire 1966-1967 season, but suddenly found himself, like his immediate predecessors, on shaky ground. Finally, after 37 games, general manager Eddie Donovan decided to make a change, and with it, he was changing the Knicks' fortunes. Donovan named William "Red" Holzman as the team's new coach.

Holzman was a 48-year-old basketball lifer in 1968, a native New Yorker who grew up with the sport. He was an All-Scholastic New York City choice in 1938 and a three-time All-American under the legendary Nat Holman at City College of New York from 1940-1942. After a stint in the Navy during World War II, Holzman immediately returned to basketball. He played with the NBL Rochester Royals from 1945-1948, then came into the NBA with the Royals and continued his playing career with the team through 1953. Playing for and with basketball legends such as Les Harrison, Al Cervi, and Bob Davies, Holzman was part of two Royals championship teams in 1946 and 1951, while learning all there was to know about the game as it was played back then.

His coaching career began when he was named player/coach of the Milwaukee Hawks in 1953. A year later he became the full-time coach and stayed with the team when it moved to St. Louis in 1955 and right through the 1957 season. Though Holzman's record with the Hawks was just 83-120, he is credited with helping in the development of great Hawks forward Bob Pettit. One year after Holzman left, the Hawks won their only NBA title. By then, Holzman became a Knicks assistant and stayed in that role until Donovan elevated him to head man in the middle of the 1967-1968 season.

SEE THE BALL, DAMMIT

Red Holzman had a saying that expressed a philosophy that he would never abandon. "If you play good, hard defense," he would say, "the offense will take care of itself." He fully believed that, having grown up with a game that stressed both ball and player movement. Before the days of the jump shot, it was much more difficult for a player to get that good look at the hoop, making it necessary for the offensive players to work harder to lose their defender, and at the same time requiring the defender to work his tail off to keep up. Holzman still believed in that kind of game—disrupt the offense in every possible way and do it for 48 minutes a game. No easy baskets, few uncontested shots, steal the ball, tip it away, but most importantly keep your eye on it constantly.

During his early practices he began implementing his philosophy, and those watching would hear him bark out time and again. SEE THE BALL! SEE THE BALL, WILLIS! SEE IT,

BRADLEY. SEE THE BALL, DAMMIT, SEE IT, SEE IT! Over and over again until it drove the players nuts. But Holzman wanted it done his way. There was no alternative, no choice. If he was going to succeed in building the Knicks into a winner, it would be done his way and with his philosophical bent.

Holzman wanted to create a mindset where his players would go on defense the instant after they scored a basket. He felt that a player's natural inclination was to relax for a few seconds when he or his teammates scored, maybe even raising his arms or high-fiving a teammate, and sometimes even looking at the crowd for its approval. He wanted none of that. You score and you go on defense. Bam! Just like that. He wanted his defenders to backpedal down the court when they could, watching the ball and trying to intercept or deflect it whenever the offensive team made a pass. The new coach had obviously seen what Bill Russell's defense had done for the Celtics, and while the Knicks didn't have a player with Russell's speed, timing, or dexterity, he felt they could create the same kind of havoc as a team. He wanted the Knicks to create a situation in which opposing teams feared their defensive ability. He wanted the ball-handler to always be aware of the defenders around him, to think twice before throwing a pass, and to play with the kind of hesitancy that would throw off the team's rhythm. And that's why he drilled his team so hard.

Red Holzman was determined to make his second tenure as a coach a successful one, and he would do whatever it took to make sure that happened.

CAN IT WORK?

Practices under Holzman became what they should be—hard work. Cries of SEE THE BALL! rang out constantly, as did HIT THE OPEN MAN! when he paid attention to the offense.

Red Holzman's philosophy was perfect for Walt Frazier. The two were made for each other and once Holzman became head coach, Frazier became an NBA superstar.
AP/WWP

Holzman was not only trying to improve the Knicks immediately, he was also evaluating what he had, looking at the potential of the players on the floor and what they might become under his guiding hand. Eventually he would have to decide who could stay and who had to go, and just what he would need to bring in to create the balance and the team chemistry that he wanted.

The rookie Frazier, for example, had looked like another draft-choice bust the first part of the season. He seemed lost on the court, not sure how to run the team, get his shot, or work with his teammates. He was already hearing it from the fans and would admit later, "I really played lousy at first." Frazier wasn't even playing half the game, splitting time with Butch Komives and Emmett Bryant at point guard. But once Holzman took over, Frazier's game began to improve. Defense had always been one of his strong suits, and with a coach who put so much emphasis on it, the rookie guard felt more relaxed and confident. He had a coach who didn't expect him to score 20 a game, just play great defense and run the offense efficiently. Anything else would be a bonus.

Reed, however, was having another outstanding season. Because he had been around the team since Reed's rookie year, Holzman already knew the big guy's qualities and what he could ultimately do for the Knicks. There wasn't a player around the league who didn't respect Reed—and maybe even fear him a little—because everyone knew what had happened between Willis and the Los Angeles Lakers in 1965-1966, Reed's second year in the league. The Knicks were playing the Lakers shortly after the trade that brought Walt Bellamy to New York. Reed was at power forward and guarding the veteran Laker, Rudy LaRusso.

"Rudy was doing a lot of pushing and shoving that night," Reed would say later. "He was continually climbing my back to get to the ball. When I told the ref to watch him, he looked at me as if I was nuts. That's when I told him, 'If you don't take care of it, I will.'"

Minutes later after an exchange of elbows, LaRusso took a wild swing at Reed, and that's when Willis knew what he had to do. "Just because he was a veteran, he didn't have the right to abuse me that way," he said. "I'm just as much a man, and if I had to pay a fine for my pride, I'd do it. Sometimes a man has to establish himself as a man."

In the next few seconds Willis totally cleaned house. He hit LaRusso with two shots in the mouth, then knocked opposing center Darrell Imhoff to the floor, and after that broke L.A. forward John Block's nose. When order was restored, Willis Reed had established himself as a player you didn't mess with. He even warned his own teammates, telling them if a fight ever broke out they should not attempt to restrain him, explaining he was once hit with a bottle in college as his teammates restrained him. In effect, he said to his teammates if they tried to restrain him in a fight he would deck them, too. Coach Holzman, who had been around since the rough-and-tumble early days of the NBA, knew then that Reed was his kind of player.

Bellamy was another story. The big guy's numbers were down again, and Holzman had to notice his on-and-off performances. The coach wanted players who would bring it every night. Russell was scoring more and adjusting to the NBA game, but he would never quite play the kind of team and defensive game Holzman wanted. Yet his natural talent made him a valuable piece. Barnett was a wily veteran who could adopt, and Holzman saw him as a shooting guard who could get the job done, and an underrated defensive player, as well.

Then there was Bradley. It was becoming apparent that he would not be the same kind of superstar in the NBA that he was in college. But Holzman saw his work ethic and all-around court savvy. He felt Bradley could fit into his concept if he surrounded him with the right players. It might not happen next week, or even next year, but the coach believed it would happen. Another player Holzman liked was 6'7" rookie Phil Jackson. The square-shouldered Jackson had long arms and knew how to use them defensively. He didn't score a lot but could be a valuable addition off the bench.

Under Holzman, the Knicks were immediately a better team. In fact, they became winners right away under the coach's constant prodding. After a 15-22 start, Holzman brought them in at 28-17, giving them a 43-39 record for the year, their first winning season since 1958-1959. They finished third behind Philadelphia and Boston in the East, making the playoffs. But they still weren't strong enough. The 76ers eliminated them in the first round in six games.

Reed led the way, averaging 20.8 points and 13.2 rebounds. Barnett averaged 18.0 points, Russell 16.9, and Bellamy 16.7, his lowest mark since coming into the league. The rookie Frazier averaged 9.0 points and a team-high 305 assists. Bradley, however, played in just 45 games and averaged only eight points. The Knicks were just one of five teams that year to score more than they gave up, so Holzman's influence was being felt. The question still remained whether this bunch could challenge for a title or if further changes had to be made.

CHAPTER 3

THE TRADE HEARD 'ROUND THE LEAGUE

SAME OL', SAME OL'

In 1968-1969, the league expanded from 12 to 14 teams with the addition of the Milwaukee Bucks and Phoenix Suns. The Knicks lost the versatile Dick Van Arsdale to expansion, and their number-one draft pick was a 6'8" forward, Bill Hosket, of Ohio State. There were some other changes, as well, most of them bench players. Rookie forward Don May of Dayton joined the team as did guard Mike Riordan. Nate Bowman, a thin 6'10" center who hadn't played much the year before, was also back. Komives and Barnett started in the backcourt with Russell, Reed, and Bellamy up front, and Frazier serving as the third guard. After the team had finished so strongly the year before, optimistic fans packed the Garden, looking forward to better things.

There was also evidence that the balance of power was changing. Though the Celtics had won once again the year before, their 10th title in 12 years, there were signs the dynasty might be done. Bill Russell would be 35 years old by the time the playoffs rolled around, and while the supporting cast was still strong (John Havlicek, Bailey Howell, Satch Sanders, Sam Jones), Russell remained the key. Philadelphia was still strong, but now without Wilt Chamberlain, who has been dealt to the Los Angeles Lakers. The Baltimore Bullets, on the other hand, were coming on. In 1967 they drafted a high-scoring guard out of Winston-Salem named Earl "The Pearl" Monroe. Now, they had picked a 6'8" hulk of a center named Wes Unseld out of Louisville. Unseld would prove himself an instant star, an outstanding defender and rebounder with the uncanny instinct of throwing quick and accurate outlet passes to start the fastbreak. So the Eastern Division would still be a tossup. Hopefully, the Knicks would be right in the mix.

LOSING AND GRIPING GO HAND IN HAND

At the outset of the 1968-1969 season, the Knicks began losing. It's the good old Knicks again, thought their cynical fans. Here was a new coach, a new system, young players being worked into the lineup, a team coming off a winning season and outstanding second half...and they were losing again. But nothing is exactly how it seems. Despite Coach Holzman's exhortations at practice and during games, there was still something missing. It's called chemistry, and it still wasn't there. All the players on a winning team don't have to like each other. Witness the Oakland A's in the early 1970s and the Yankees of 1977-1978. These were baseball teams with larger rosters, but comprised of guys who often antagonized and battled each other, but on the field came together to battle the opposition and won.

With the Knicks, it was something else. The grousing and internal bickering were affecting the way the team performed on the court. For openers, Howard Komives, who was still seeing considerable time at point guard, never got along with Cazzie

Russell. Their long-standing animosity sometimes resulted in Komives not giving Russell the ball every time he should, even when Russell was obviously open. This had started long before Holzman took over the team, and even the coach's repeated "HIT THE OPEN MAN" orders didn't change things.

It was also becoming obvious that Walt Bellamy simply was not the right man in the middle to put Holzman's philosophies into practice. There was little doubt that when he came to play, Big Bells had the talent to compete with almost anyone. But the key phrase was *when he came to play*. Everyone knew that he didn't come to play every night. and it was becoming more apparent that it wasn't going to change. There were times when Bellamy stood there as if his sneakers were nailed to the floor while a player of lesser talent drove right past him to the hoop. To make matters worse, Bellamy's expression on the court rarely changed. He didn't show emotion, didn't exhort his teammates, and the impression everyone got from all this was that he didn't really care. One player put it this way:

"Bellamy was like an anchor tied to a sailing ship. When other guys were yelling, 'Let's go, let's go,' Walt would say nothing. Yet he was a sensitive guy, and I don't think he sensed there was respect for him as a player from the other guys on the team."

In many ways it appeared that Bellamy was a guy who went through the motions. When there was a Chamberlain or a Russell to challenge him, he responded. But he really didn't play much defense and didn't appear to want to. It was like a guy in a dead-end nine-to-five job. He showed up, put in his time, and went home. He never gave you any extra. With Bellamy, the Knicks might still compile a winning record, but it didn't appear he was the guy who would help take them to a championship.

The team lost 13 of its first 19 games, and thoughts of a winning season quickly began receding over the horizon. Holzman and GM Eddie Donovan called several team meetings to try to ferret out the problems. A couple of guys complained about their playing time, but that was to be expected. Since only five guys can be on the court at once, someone is always grousing about that. Bill Bradley, the consummate team player, who was showing great improvement from his aborted rookie year, said that too many guys were still going one on one and not fully embracing the team game that Holzman had espoused. And a number of players said flat-out that the team could not become part of the top echelon in the league without the right big man in the middle, a direct reference to you-know-who.

And that's when Holzman and Donovan looked to make a move, a trade that would not only improve the team, but one that would also bring the team closer together. Ironically, as coach and GM began looking around the league, the club began playing better basketball, slowly easing closer to the .500 mark. But that didn't deter the two from still looking to make a deal. If it seemed the right one for the team, they would pull the trigger.

DECEMBER 19, 1968, A DAY THAT WILL LIVE IN NEW YORK HISTORY

When you're looking to make a trade, you usually have to give something to get something. Both teams must feel the deal will improve their records and their working chemistry at the same time. A player swap also has to fill certain needs for the current situation. Sometimes, then, it depends on the state of the team. A club going nowhere might be more prone to deal a star player for a couple of guys who will help with rebuilding, especially since the star isn't going to be happy in a dead-end situation. And that's what made the Knicks look at the Detroit Pistons.

The trade that changed the history of the Knicks forever brought rugged forward Dave DeBusschere (22) to the team on December 19, 1968. DeBusschere was the final piece to the Knicks championship puzzle.
Photo by Vernon J. Biever

The Pistons were that team going nowhere. They hadn't had a winning season since 1955-1956, when the franchise was still located in Fort Wayne, Indiana. They had also had four coaches in five years, usually the mark of a franchise in disarray. There was, however, one player whom the Knicks were eying, not only because of his basketball acumen, but because of the circumstances in Detroit. They felt he could be had if the price was right.

Dave DeBusschere was a 6'6", 225-pound forward with diverse skills, a physical and cerebral player alike. He was also a local hero in Detroit, having been born in the motor city on October 16, 1940. After starring in both baseball and basketball at Austin Catholic High, DeBusschere turned down offers from much larger colleges to stay home and attend the University of Detroit. He averaged 24.8 points a game with the basketball team, which made it to the NCAA tournament one year and the NIT two other times. He was also a star pitcher on the baseball team, leading them into the NCAA tourney on three occasions. By that time, there wasn't a single sports fan in Detroit who didn't know and admire Dave DeBusschere.

When DeBusschere graduated in 1962, baseball was a much bigger sport than basketball, both financially and in popularity. But he also loved the hardwood game and became one of the few athletes to attempt the balancing act of playing both. He received a $75,000 signing bonus from the Chicago White Sox, then became a territorial pick of the Pistons and signed a $15,000, one-year deal to play for them. He immediately showed promise in both sports. As a rookie with the Pistons, DeBusschere averaged 12.7 points a game and grabbed 694 rebounds, making the NBA's all-rookie team. There was little doubt he could make his mark in the NBA.

With baseball, it normally takes longer to reach the majors. DeBusschere stuck it out for three years. He had 25-9 record in two years pitching for the White Sox Triple-A farm club at

Indianapolis in 1964 and 1965, and had a couple of brief stints in the majors before that. In 1962 he appeared in 12 games for the Sox, and a year later he was in 24, starting 10. He had a 3-4 record and 3.09 earned run average in 84 1/3 innings in 1963, striking out 53 while walking 34. He also threw a complete-game shutout. On the mound, DeBusschere was a hard-throwing right hander with obvious promise, but the Sox kept him in the minors the next two years and after 1965 he finally gave up baseball to concentrate on basketball, saying, "I knew I'd have to choose sooner or later."

And no wonder. Besides becoming an outstanding player, in November of 1964 owner Fred Zollner named him player/coach of the team. He was just 24 years old and starting his third season. Now, a guy who was playing two professional sports also had to coach a diverse group of guys, many older than he was, in one of them. Some said Zollner named DeBusschere coach to encourage him to give up baseball. Having a dual role wasn't easy for a number of reasons. The team wasn't that talented, and the coach didn't have a helluva lot of experience. Plus he had to concentrate on becoming a better player. He coached until there were just eight games remaining in the 1966-1967 season when he was replaced by Donnis Butcher. DeBusschere's coaching record was 79-143, and the team never made the playoffs. In the end, he was glad to have a huge weight taken from his shoulders.

"It was a relief to give up coaching," he said, in an interview some time later. "I realize now there were things I wasn't mature enough to handle. As soon as I was back on my own again, I had my best season. I was scoring better, rebounding better, defending better, and doing everything else better."

He was right. In 1967-1968, DeBusschere was the Pistons' second high scorer behind Dave Bing, averaging 17.9 points per game. He was also the team's leading rebounder with 1,081 caroms in 80 games, an average of 13.5 boards a game. That was good for eighth best in the league, just ahead of Willis Reed of the Knicks. No wonder he was the guy they wanted. In fact, the Knicks had tried to get DeBusschere before, only to be told "No way" by the Pistons. But in 1968-1969, things had changed.

Once again the Pistons had a new coach. NBA veteran Paul Seymour took over the team, and like many new coaches, Seymour wanted to put his own stamp on the ballclub. He felt the team needed an infusion of new players to break away from years of losing. Remember, to get something you have to give something. So he felt he had to deal the team's most marketable commodity—and that was Dave DeBusschere.

On December 19, the deal was made. The Knicks would get DeBusschere and at the same time were able to rid themselves of their two most difficult players. They gave the Pistons Walt Bellamy and Howard Komives. This was one trade that received universal approval everywhere throughout the Big Apple. The players loved it, the fans loved it, the media loved it, and Coach Red Holzman loved it.

THE NEW KNICKS

By trading for Dave DeBusschere, the Knicks had completely changed the face of their team in the time it took Bellamy and Komives to leave town and DeBusschere to arrive. For openers, the talented but often indifferent Bellamy was gone. The man who was supposed to give the Knicks the answer to Russell and Chamberlain but had barely given them an answer to Connie Dierking could now take his wares to Detroit. His departure would also give Willis Reed a chance to move back into the middle. Reed had always maintained he was a natural center, even while making the All-NBA Second Team as a forward the past two seasons. Now Reed, whose work ethic, hustle, and attitude were diametrically opposed to Bellamy's, would get a chance to bump heads with the best big men in the league.

But that wasn't all. With Reed moving back to center, DeBusschere would take over the forward slot, which today is called the "power" forward slot. In other words, he'd be the one to match up with the best big forwards in the league. Though three inches shorter than Willis, DeBusschere was faster and could keep up with the Elgin Baylors, Gus Johnsons, and Chet Walkers of the world. Double D. was also a tenacious rebounder who didn't mind battling and banging under the boards. At the same time, he was also a good shooter with more range on his jumper than Reed, but he could score underneath as well. So the move was definitely an upgrade at two positions.

And that still wasn't all. The departure of the often-combative Komives opened the point guard spot up for Walt Frazier. Clyde, as he would come to be known, would now get a shot full time. He was already showing marked improvement from his rookie season and now would be the man with the ball. Komives, at the time of his departure, was still playing 26 minutes a game, slightly more than half, so now everyone concerned would be able to see just what the second-year guard out of Southern Illinois could do. After Komives's departure, it would be difficult to get Frazier off the floor.

Cazzie Russell was getting the majority of time at the other forward spot, the small forward, and was averaging around 18 points a game. Russell was a streak shooter capable of scoring points in bunches. Though not a consummate defender, the team felt they could cover his mistakes with the new alignment, and Bill Bradley, who was playing between 15 and 20 minutes a game, was showing marked improvement over his rookie season and proving to be extremely coachable. He followed Holzman's concepts to a tee.

The new Knicks took to the floor just a night after the trade was completed. In a real touch of irony, their opponents were the Detroit Pistons, with Bellamy and Komives in the lineup. One only had to look at the final score to see which team got the better of the deal. The Knicks won it by 48 points, 135-87. It was the largest margin of victory in club history. A new era had truly begun.

FROM THE MEDIOCRE TO THE ELITE

The big win over Detroit wasn't a fluke. The dramatic trade has completed the picture that Holzman was trying to paint. He now had the team he wanted. DeBusschere fit into the lineup like a smooth-as-silk glove. Reed was back in his natural position, doing all the physical things that Bellamy couldn't or wouldn't do, while Walt Frazier was suddenly looking like an all-pro on defense and also showing something many people thought his game lacked—offense. The veteran Barnett was steady as a rock, a cool presence who continued to hit his unorthodox left-handed jumper while showing a surprising proclivity to play good defense. He, too, had a total game. It took Red Holzman and the right teammates to bring it out.

Then, in January, with the team already winning, fate took a hand and made the equation even better. The Knicks were playing the Seattle Supersonics and handling them with ease. Suddenly, there was a collision between Cazzie Russell and Seattle sub Joe Kennedy. Both players went down hard, Kennedy falling on top of Cazzie's legs. He got up, but Russell didn't. Cazzie sat there clutching his right ankle and in obvious pain. Russell was helped from the court, and when the news came down it wasn't good. His ankle was broken and he'd be out for most of, if not all of the regular season. Ordinarily, that would have been a sharp blow to a team just finding itself. As it turned out, Cazzie's bad break was a good one for the Knicks.

Enter Bill Bradley. Dollar Bill had been waiting patiently for his chance, working hard, refining his game, getting his basketball legs back after his sojourn at Oxford. He loved the team concept that Holzman had fostered and also welcomed the acquisition of DeBusschere. Once he was in the starting lineup it became apparent almost immediately that the team was a bit smoother, a bit sharper, a bit tougher defensively. It wasn't a knock on Russell. Cazzie's offensive game could help almost any team, but with the Knicks it would probably be better served coming off the bench. Most ardent Knick fans knew almost immediately that even when Cazzie returned, he would assume the role of sixth man, maybe even do what Boston's great sixth men—Frank Ramsey and later John Havlicek—had done for their team, providing a spark via instant offense.

After the trade the Knicks simply took off, playing as well as any team in the league. They ran off a 10-game winning streak from December 17, through January 4, and then topped it by winning 11 in a row between January 25, and February 15. Opposing teams were suddenly taking notice. This was no longer the same old Knicks, a team that would more often than not find a way to lose. They were a team to be reckoned with, a tough ballclub that battled right down to the final buzzer and gave no quarter to anyone. When the 1968-1969 season ended, the Knicks had a 54-28 record and were sitting in third place in the Eastern Division, just three games behind Baltimore and one behind Philadelphia. They had also finished six games ahead of the 48-34 Boston Celtics, a team that seemed to be finally fading as Bill Russell aged. Even more impressive was the fact that the Knicks were 36-11 following the trade for DeBusschere that allowed them to finish with the fourth best record in the entire NBA. Had DeBusschere been there since game one, there's no doubt they would have had the league's best mark.

All that then posed a very logical question. Was this team good enough to win the championship? And win it now?

DISAPPOINTMENT TEMPERED BY OPTIMISM

Individually, a number of Knicks had really excelled during the season. Reed, playing most of the year back at center, led the team with a 21.1 scoring average. Willis was also seventh in the league in rebounding with 1,191 caroms and a 14.5 average. Barnett averaged 17.6 points a game, while Frazier surprised everyone by raising his average to 17.5 after becoming a full-time point guard. He also had 635 assists, a 7.9 average that was third best in the league behind the great Oscar Robertson and Lennie Wilkens of Seattle. DeBusschere average 16.3 points and 11.7 rebounds and did all the little things—the intangibles—that helped make the Knicks an elite team. And Bradley, with a chance to really see some court time, had his scoring average up to 12.4 and was second on the team with 302 assists, showing the kind of team player and passer he was. Russell, as mentioned earlier, was coming into his own as a scorer before his injury and averaged 18.3 points in 50 games.

Both Reed and DeBusschere were named to the All-NBA second team. And for the first time ever, the league decided to pick an All-Defensive team. In addition to Bill Russell, Nate Thurmond, and Jerry Sloan, the final two slots were filled by Walt Frazier and the aforementioned DeBusschere. Because of those two as well as the rest of the team, Coach Holzman's defensive concepts had also paid off. With the right combination of players in place, the Knicks allowed a league-low 105.2 points a game.

So when the playoffs began, there was no reason to think the Knicks wouldn't be in the thick of it. And when they swept the high-scoring, first-place Baltimore Bullets in four straight games, it began to look as if the Knicks were becoming a juggernaut. Then, in the division finals, they suddenly found themselves up against an old nemesis. The Boston Celtics, a team that appeared old and vulnerable during the regular season, had suddenly come to life and defeated the Philadelphia 76ers in just five games in their opening round. Yet there was still no reason to panic. In the regular season the Knicks had beaten the Celtics six of the seven times the two teams played. They went in the favorites.

Then something unexpected happened. The Celtics, a team that still had a fine supporting cast around Russell, began turning back the clock again. It was as if Russell, who was player/coach and planning to retire, had made this a personal challenge for he and his team to rise to the occasion one last time. They won the opener at Madison Square Garden, 108-100. Then, in the second game at the Boston Garden, it was like old times. Despite the return of Cazzie Russell, it was the other Russell who dominated. Big Bill grabbed 21 rebounds in the first half alone and led his club to an easy, 112-97 win, and a 2-0 lead in the series. It might as well have been over right there.

The Knicks rallied to win the third game, but when the Celts took Game 4, giving them a 3-1 lead, they were clearly in the driver's seat. The Knicks managed to win Game 5 in New York, but Frazier suffered a groin injury in the final minute. He played in Game 6, but was obviously not able to go at full speed. In fact, before the game Willis Reed was purported to have said, "I took one look at Clyde and knew we were out of it." But they battled, finally going down by a single point, 106-105, and the Celtics— not the favored Knicks—were in the final.

Boston would go on to top the Los Angeles Lakers in seven games to win its 11th championship in 13 years, a record unsurpassed in all of sports. Russell then made good on his word and retired, forever the ultimate champion. Thus, when the 1969-1970 season approached, the NBA was ripe for a new champion. The Knicks had produced the best record in the league from the day Dave DeBusschere arrived and they had to be the preseason favorite. But the New Yorkers didn't look at it that way. In their minds, it was a matter of unfinished business.

They wanted to complete the mission they had begun on the previous December 20. And they felt they now had the horses to do it.

CHAPTER 4

A NEW SEASON AND A STREAK TO REMEMBER

THE CAST OF CHARACTERS

There were some changes in the balance of NBA power going into the 1969-1970 season. Russell was gone, quickly relegating the Celtics to the unfamiliar role of also-rans. The Bullets still had their swift-striking offensive team but didn't have the defensive prowess of the Knicks. In the West, Atlanta was good and would wind up acquiring old pal Walt Bellamy late in the season, but they were not considered a team that could close it out with a title. Then there was the Los Angeles Lakers. L.A. had an aging trio of superstars—Jerry West, Elgin Baylor, and Wilt Chamberlain—but only West was still operating at peak efficiency. Baylor, the acrobatic, high-scoring forward, was often hurt now, and Wilt...well, he was still Wilt, but that had only translated into a title once, back in 1966-1967 with Philadelphia.

More eyes this year would probably be on the Milwaukee Bucks, a team that was just in its second season of existence. That was because the Bucks had the first draft choice in the league in early 1969 and used it to pick 7'2" center Lew Alcindor out of UCLA. Alcindor, who would change his name a year later to Kareem Abdul-Jabbar, had a brilliant collegiate career and was an offensive force, his repertoire highlighted by an unstopping "sky" hook. Whether he could turn the Bucks around in his first year remained to be seen.

As for the Knicks, they were starting the year with essentially the same cast of characters that had finished the season before so strongly. Russell was back, but Bradley was now ensconced as the starter with Cazzie coming off the bench. The only rookie was John Warren, a guard out of St. John's, but he wouldn't see much action. Mike Riordan, a self-made player with a huge work ethic, would spell Frazier when necessary and could also be used to give Barnett a breather. Nate Bowman, Bill Hosket, and Don May were all back, but their minutes would be limited. The biggest surprise, and one that would help, was the return of Dave Stallworth. Dave the Rave has missed two full seasons after suffering what doctors said was a mild heart attack. Whatever it was, Stallworth was back with full medical clearance, and his return negated the one loss. Phil Jackson, whose defense was loved by Coach Holzman, was lost for the season due to back surgery. Otherwise, however, the team led by their captain, Willis Reed, was intact and ready to make a run at the first championship in franchise history.

WHO SAID THE NBA WAS BIG TIME?

Even though the team had finished with that great 36-11 rush the season before, Coach Holzman treated practice sessions as if he were drilling a team of kindergarteners. Cries of SEE THE BALL! SEE THE BALL! continued to echo in the empty gym when the team worked out. When they scrimmaged, the coach was more critical, often yelling, GET YOUR ASS BACK

Forward Dave Stallworth (9) returned to the team after missing two seasons with a heart ailment and gave the Knicks speed and scoring off the bench.
Photo by Vernon J. Biever

ON DEFENSE! PICK UP YOUR MAN, DAMMIT! I DON'T
WANT TO SEE ANY OPEN SHOTS! He would say it more
than once, often repeating it until his commands seemed to be
coming from a series of broken records. The players were also
learning to communicate with each other, calling out picks and
switches, as well as cues to where the ball was or where it was
going. The goal was to make the five defenders think as one, and
it was working. The sweet taste of success that the team cooked
up after the DeBusschere trade made everyone hunger for more.
Only this time the goal wasn't modest; it was greedy. They
wanted it all. The Knicks wanted that championship.

The rookies in training camp where just bodies, fodder for
practice sessions. Everyone pretty much knew who would be on
the roster once the season began. When someone asked Dave
DeBusschere about some of the first-year players, he gave a
surprising answer. "I'll be honest with you," he said, "I don't even
know their names. I don't know they're here. Why become
attached to somebody when you have a pretty good idea they're
not going to be around long?"

It wasn't that DeBusschere was being snobbish or standoffish.
It was just the reality of the NBA. There's not much room on a
12-man roster when 11 of those 12 spots are already set. Frazier,
on the other hand, made it his business to know their names,
though he was as realistic as DeBusschere about their chances of
sticking. Just two years removed from being a rookie himself, he
knew how good it felt when a veteran called him by name. So his
approach was a bit different. But basically, all the veterans went
through the motions at the small gym in Farmingdale, Long
Island, with one purpose in mind—to get ready for the season.

Once the preseason games began, the team began to get a
better feel for each other and for the competition. But they didn't
get a feel for big crowds. During these warmup contests it was as
if the league turned back the clock and sent its teams back into
the 1940s. One reason was that the league arenas were often

booked for other events then. They had to keep the revenue flowing. As mentioned, there were even times in earlier years when the Knicks couldn't use Madison Square Garden for some of their playoff games because the circus was in town. So back in 1969, teams were almost sent off on a barnstorming tour to play their exhibition games.

The Knicks' schedule sent them to places like Saginaw and Grand Rapids in Michigan, Paterson and Trenton, New Jersey; Bethlehem, Pennsylvania; Utica, New York; and Bangor, Maine. It almost sounded like the early days of the NBL when there were teams in places like Waterloo and Sheboygan. It's amazing the Knicks didn't have a game scheduled for Tri-Cities! In fact, in those real early days of the NBA, Knicks president Ned Irish always watched which teams would come to town. If it was the Boston Celtics you might see BOSTON CELTICS HERE TONIGHT on the front marquee of the old Garden. But if it was a team like the Anderson Packers or Waterloo Hawks, the marquee would probably read, PROFESSIONAL BASKETBALL HERE TONIGHT. There was still a degree of embarrassment over the small-townish feel of the league then. The Knicks' exhibition season must have made it feel like these good old days. Heck, in some of those places the players might have found a hook in place of a locker.

But it was still basketball. The courts were 94 feet long, and the baskets 10 feet high. So it was a way to get ready. The team played 10 preseason games and didn't worry too much about winning and losing. It was simply a time to refine the system, and that's what they did, winning six and losing four. Everyone was pointing to opening night. And, in a way, DeBusschere was right. All the rookies he didn't want to get to know were gone, except for John Warren. He would join Hosket, May, and Bowman at the end of the bench. The regular-season rotation would be pretty much the five starters, then Russell, Stallworth, and Riordan. The others would only play in one-sided victories or defeats, or in emergency situations. The team was hanging its hat on the first eight guys. They held the keys to the team's success in their hands.

DEFENSE, DEFENSE, DEFENSE

The Boston Celtics always excelled defensively because of one man—Bill Russell. Sure, the supporting cast was damned good, and players like "Satch" Sanders, John Havlicek, and K.C. Jones could also be defensive demons. But Russell was the great equalizer. Another player could gamble on making a steal or intercepting a pass knowing full well that the big guy had his back. If an offensive player got past his man and started into the paint or drove toward the hoop, he'd have to contend with Russell's speed, instincts, wingspan, and uncanny ability to block shots. That was one of the main ingredients that made the Celtics great.

The Knicks didn't have a Bill Russell. Reed, in his own right, was an outstanding center, a rugged rebounder and a policeman on the court who commanded total respect all around the league. In a nutshell, no one really wanted to mess with Willis. Everyone knew how he had cleaned up on the Lakers years earlier, and that reputation helped him command the middle of the floor. But he wasn't a great shotblocker and didn't have great speed. No, for the Knicks to be effective defensively, it had to be a total team effort, and that's what Holzman and his players worked to achieve.

The first line of defense for the Knicks was to disrupt the normal flow of the ball-handler. They did this by trying to force him to spots on the floor where he didn't really want to go and where he would be more susceptible to a double-team and possible steal. If they couldn't get the steal they would try to force an errant or ill-advised pass. If nothing else, this would disrupt the flow of the opposition's offense. Both Frazier and Barnett were crafty and becoming more adept at working this kind of defensive magic. They concentrated on driving the ball handler toward the sideline and as close to the corner as they could. By doing this, they would create separation between the ball handler and the recipient of an intended pass. This kind of maneuvering would then disrupt the flow and balance of the offense

Because Frazier was more adept at making the steal, he was often assigned to the weaker guard, while Barnett took the star. Clyde would only take the team's best for brief stretches or against certain teams where the matchups dictated it. Frazier also stayed a bit farther away from the man he was guarding than most defenders. He had the knack of beating them to the spot and often lulled them into a sense of false security by the distance he kept. As a rule, only a shotblocker like Bill Russell would lay back and swoop in at the last second. Frazier did this from his guard position. And when he finally went for the ball he often picked their pockets and left them with a look of surprise. Just as Cazzie Russell was a streak shooter on offense, Frazier's adrenaline was often sparked by his defense, and he would often become a "streak thief," nabbing the ball two, three, or four times in succession. And he loved it.

"I'm sort of like a dope addict," he once said. "I can't stay away from the ball. After I've made one steal, I'm really keyed up. For the next three or four minutes I must just go wild, in spurts. I love to hear the cheers of the crowd. It really psyches me up, and I think my steals help psych the Garden up, too."

Frazier's dedication to the "D" began his sophomore year at Southern Illinois when he was declared academically ineligible for a short time. When he came back, he was mostly used as a defensive body in practice to work against the regulars. He took this as a personal challenge and made it his business to make the regulars look as bad as he possibly could. "We tried to humiliate them," was the way he put it. Soon, he realized that playing great defense gave him a tremendous amount of satisfaction, and it stayed with him after he joined the Knicks.

DeBusschere was another outstanding defender, a guy who never stopped working at the defensive end. It was his job to stop the hotshot forwards in the league, whether they did it through finesse or strength. While he didn't do anything flashy, those playing against him suddenly found themselves struggling, having an off night. But the off night was often created by the hard work being put in by DeBusschere. He was especially adept at keeping his offensive man from getting the ball, and when you don't have the ball you can't score. Dave also worked the boards with the determination of a man who felt it was a personal failure when he didn't come up with the basketball. Having him up front took some of the pressure off of Reed.

Bradley did not have the look of a tenacious defender. He wasn't as strong as many of the players he was matched up against and couldn't jump as well. He was also shorter, at 6'5", than most of the players he would be guarding. Yet Bradley was smart and quick. Teams that tried to lob passes over his head often found that strategy would eventually disrupt their offense. When his man got the ball closer to the corners, Bradley used his ability to keep his man from getting the pass off and could often disrupt the dribble with his quick hands.

"Red was one of the first coaches to see that when a big guy takes a smaller man into the pivot, it's not necessarily an advantage," Bradley said. "Other teams see it as a mismatch, but if the forward is not the big scorer, sometimes this just disrupts the offense."

Reed, though no Bill Russell, could surprise by blocking a shot when the shooter least expected it. He was also both an enforcer and a guy with the ability to anticipate the ball coming into the middle. He would often step out suddenly and prevent a smaller shooter from taking one from just behind the foul circle. Underneath, opponents knew when Reed went for the ball. Like DeBusschere, he went after rebounds with a take-no-prisoners mentality and used his considerable bulk to send a message to those who decided to bump bodies with him. As Reed so indelicately put it:

"In this game you're out there for the kill with the objective being to win."

The other players, with the exception of the always-working, always-moving Mike Riordan, didn't have quite the same defensive prowess as the starters, but when the Knicks regulars had it going, the chants of "DEE-FENSE! DEE-FENSE! DEE-FENSE!" always came cascading down from the upper reaches of the Garden.

NO SLOW START THIS TIME

On October 14, it all became real. The Knicks opened the regular season at Madison Square Garden in front of a full house of just more than 19,500 fans. The Sonics were an expansion team in just their third year of existence. Their best player was probably their coach, the veteran guard Lenny Wilkens, who had taken over just this year and was coaching his first game. His team, however, simply didn't have the horses to stay with the Knicks. Right from the start the Knicks' defensive philosophy had the Sonics completely out of sync. Frazier and Barnett completely took the game away from Wilkens and his backcourt partner, Art Harris. They forced them out of their patterns, double-teamed, swiped at the ball, stole it, created fouls and turnovers.

At one point, Wilkens was so intent on watching the predatory Frazier that he charged into the stationary Barnett for a foul. Minutes later, Frazier went after Harris from behind, trying to poke the ball away. He missed, but the maneuver distracted Harris enough that Barnett stepped across and made the steal. It was like that all night. At the other end, the Knicks scored often and made the game a runaway. It was over by the third quarter, and Holzman made sure all his players got a taste of the early action. The Knicks won handily, 126-101, a preview of things to come. The team that had played so well the season before after dealing for Dave DeBusschere looked better than ever. What's more, they had quickly sent a message to the rest of the league. This Knicks team was for real.

The next night the team topped the Cincinnati Royals, who were now being coached by the great Bob Cousy, 94-89, then had another laugher against the Chicago Bulls, 116-87. Against the Lakers, Frazier was guarding rookie Willie McCarter, while Barnett had the team's incumbent star, Jerry West. The tone was set early when McCarter ran toward West as if to take a short pass. That enabled Frazier to drift over with him. Coach Joe Mullaney saw it coming and tried to warn his rookie, but as soon as Frazier got close enough he made a quick thrust, poked the ball away from West, and the Knicks had another steal. When the game ended, they also had another victory, albeit a close one, 99-96. An easy, 140-116 win over Phoenix ran the team's record to 5-0, but then the team was surprised at the Garden by a mediocre Golden State team, 112-109, for their first defeat of the season. But they had already taken hold of first place in the NBA East, and in the coming weeks they would tighten it into a stranglehold.

WITH ALL THE DEFENSE, WHAT ABOUT THE OFFENSE?

There was no question about the Knicks' defensive ability, but they had also scored big in a couple of games, so they were getting it at the other end as well. None of the Knicks was considered a great offensive player, but all of them had enough ability to put the ball in the hole to make it work as a team. Russell could score in bunches when he got the hot hand. Barnett, too, could hit a ton of his left-handed jumpers when he began to feel it. DeBusschere had proven in Detroit that he could score from both in close and the outside, and while Bradley was improving on the offensive end, it was already apparent he wouldn't be the offensive force he had been at Princeton. But he, too, could break out and post a big scoring game every now and then. Besides, scoring wasn't his primary role on this team.

Frazier and Reed had emerged as the most consistent scorers on the team. With Willis it was expected. He had been tossing in between 20-22 points consistently since his rookie year. Frazier, however, was the surprise. His offensive game looked nearly non-existent the first half of his rookie year. Once Holzman took the coaching reins and the team traded for DeBusschere, Clyde's offense began to catch up with his defense. He wasn't like Jerry West, who could flick his jumper off in the blink of an eye, but he had learned how to get his shot, and the jumper kept improving. Defenders couldn't play up on him because he had a quick, long first step that enabled him to get past them and go to the hoop. By his third year Clyde had a diverse offensive game, and the result was that he had become a 20-point scorer.

The Knicks, however, were not a run-and-gun team like the Bullets, Pistons, Lakers, and several others. They didn't have the kind of players who could often create their own shots, guys who could go one on one with any defender and more often than not beat him. Super scorers like Robertson, West, Baylor, Earl "The Pearl" Monroe were all great one-on-one players, but the Knicks needed a little help, and that meant a series of set plays.

The Knicks often worked off preset patterns to create open shots, done so effortlessly that some watching thought they were using a kind of improvised offense. They weren't. Most of the Knicks shooters had favorite spots from which to launch the basketball, and they worked on cutting and moving so they could get there, ball in hand, for an open shot. Bradley, for instance, wasn't particularly adept at getting his own shot, because ballhandling wasn't one of his strong suits. He was smart enough to know that, however, and got himself into the kind of condition that would allow constant, perpetual movement in order to shake loose from his defender. Once he got the ball with an opening, he could put it up quickly.

On one play, Frazier would take the ball down the side of the court while Bradley moved quickly along the baseline from a spot in the corner. But before he reached the other side of the court he would stop and turn quickly, then loop back to take the ball behind Frazier, who would then set the screen that would allow Bradley to take his jumper. Another play called for him to break off a double screen that DeBusschere and Reed set at the bottom of the foul lane. He made the move quickly, using a couple of quick fakes to freeze the defender, and then would get a pass from one of the guards as soon as he came around the screen. Instant jumper. Beginning to get the picture?

The Knicks also executed the classic back-door play as well as anyone. One of the forwards would come out of the corner and move toward the ball, then would suddenly spin and race toward the basket. If the defender was leaning the wrong way, a quick pass from the guards would result in an easy layup. It was basic basketball, but the Knicks would do it successfully over and over again during the course of the season.

For DeBusschere, there was something appropriately called the "D" play. Dave would receive a pass, usually from Frazier, deep on the side of the court even with the foul line. Frazier would then move toward him as if to receive a return pass. At the same time, Reed would move from the low post to a spot just outside the foul line on the same side of the court as the other two. DeBusschere would then give the ball back to Frazier then move toward Reed as if he were going to set the screen. At the last second, he would make a quick move behind Reed so that his defender would have to get around Willis. A quick pass, and he'd have an open jumper from behind Reed.

Barnett worked well with Reed at getting his jumper from the side of the court, also using the big screen set by the captain. There was a variation of the play in which Barnett would not take the shot but rather pass to one of the forwards who would move from the baseline and get the ball behind a double screen set by Frazier and the other forward. That was a play that worked very well for Cazzie Russell, who loved to launch his jumper from that spot. Reed, of course, didn't need too many plays. He could take his lefty jumper, released high over his head, from almost anywhere. He had good range for a big man and wasn't shy. If the shot was there, he'd take it.

There were other plays and variations as well. And, of course, the players were skilled enough to improvise and occasionally freelance. The more they got to know each other's court nuances, the better they became. So while the team did not have a super scorer, they had enough offensive weapons to make it all work, especially with the kind of defense they played at the other end. At the outset of the season they appeared to be a team without a weakness, one that was complete.

THE STREAK BUILDS

After losing to Golden State, the team began to win. Three straights blowouts followed—116-92 over Detroit, 128-99 against the Bullets, and 128-104 versus Atlanta. Then San Diego fell, 123-110, followed by a victory over Milwaukee and rookie Alcindor, 112-108. The Knicks had won five straight and were now 10-1 on the season. It wasn't much of a surprise that the team was already leading the league in defense. The Knicks had allowed opponents just 101.3 a game and had held opponents under 100 five times. This was at a time when teams regularly scored well over 100 points, and it was a badge of honor for the club to hold an opponent under the century mark.

At the same time, the team was winning its games by an average margin of 16.1 points. That was incredible, especially when you considered the next best team was Milwaukee, but the Bucks were only winning by an average of 4.9 points a game. The huge gap showed just how far the Knicks stood above the rest of the league at this still-early point in the season. Victories over Milwaukee, Phoenix, San Diego, and Los Angeles followed, running the team's record to 14-1 and their winning streak to nine. At Los Angeles, the Knicks did not have to face old nemesis Wilt Chamberlain. The big center had ruptured a tendon in his right kneecap, an injury that required surgery and could keep him out the rest of the season. Though Chamberlain vowed to be back for the playoffs, many thought he wouldn't make it. With Bill Russell retired and Wilt out, the League would now operate for the first time since 1956-1957 without either of the two greatest centers in league history, and that seemed to open the doors up for the Knicks even more. Reed ate up Wilt's replacement, Rick Roberson, and the team won by 10.

From there the Knicks traveled to San Francisco and avenged their only loss of the year, topping the Warriors, 116-103. DeBusschere played with an aluminum and foam protective device so he wouldn't miss time with a broken nose suffered in the Lakers game, and Reed emerged with a puffed lip from an errant elbow. But these were simply marks of the warrior, something all players faced during a long and rough season. When the team returned home and promptly beat Chicago, Boston, and Cincinnati, with the smallest margin of victory a comfortable 15 points, they had run their winning streak to 13 games and had an 18-1 mark for the season. It was a remarkable beginning, and now, a longstanding NBA record was obviously within reach.

The record for most victories in succession was 17, first set in the NBA's maiden season of 1946 by the old Washington Nationals and equaled in 1959 by the Boston Celtics. Ironically, both teams were coached by the legendary Red Auerbach. Now another Red, Holzman, had his club in pursuit of the record. That, and the fact that the Knicks were playing so well, made Madison Square Garden the place to be in New York. The Garden was often home to many celebrities from the sports, entertainment, and political worlds, in addition to an increasing number of media representatives. All kinds of people looked to get tickets, which were quickly becoming a much harder commodity to come by.

The Garden box office received numerous calls from people claiming to be relatives and friends of the players, and at the same time the scalpers thrived out on Seventh Avenue, actually holding up signs with their own private ticket prices. Not surprisingly, business was brisk. The Knicks ticket office had to install another phone line and add another secretary to handle all the requests, the legitimate ones as well as the cons, as a variety of calls and stories flooded the office, all in search of the elusive tickets. No worry about selling out. The way they were playing, the Knicks might well have sold out the Garden if it held 50,000 fans.

As for the players, they were going about business as usual. Despite the intense and prolific media coverage, none of them seemed concerned about where the streak might go. "I wasn't even aware there was a streak," Dick Barnett said, "until we got to about 15. I very seldom read the New York sports pages." As for Walt Frazier, he pointed to the fact that the Knicks were winning so easily as a reason pressure was at a minimum.

Second-year forward Donnie May didn't play a whole lot, but like the other bench players he was always ready when called upon. AP/WWP

"We didn't have that many nerve-racking games," said Clyde. "We were winning by 20 points or more, so this made it a lot easier than if we were just squeaking by. If that was the case, the pressure would begin to mount, but the way we were winning, it was no big thing."

Just a few more wins, and it would be.

WHO ARE THESE GUYS?

When a team is winning and making constant news—especially a basketball team with a limited roster—everyone thinks they know them. But even the closest knit of teams is comprised of individuals, guys who don't have to be bosom buddies off the field or the court to make it work. That's the way it was with the Knicks. They played together as well as any team of recent vintage, but off the court, the starters especially rarely hung out together. For example, both Barnett and Frazier were basically loners, but in different ways.

Barnett almost seemed to prefer a solitary kind of life. Growing up in Gary, Indiana, he once said, "I've been introverted most of my life. I never really had anybody that you could call close friends, guys who come over to your house and talk with you or stay over all night at the house." He said that he as a youngster he often attended movies alone and even practiced baseball on solitary courts. With the Knicks, he still went his own way. Surprisingly cerebral, he liked to read and had a passion for chess. He would always take a miniature chess board with him and try to solve the problems proposed in the chess columns of daily newspapers, not something you would expect from a guy with a crazy, but accurate left-handed jump shot.

Frazier was different. He was like Joe Namath without the entourage. Namath, of course, was the New York Jets quarterback and the toast of the town in 1969 after leading the Jets to their improbable victory in Super Bowl III that January. He dressed flamboyantly, often showing up at the Garden in a white fur coat and always with a crowd of friends, beautiful women, and admirers. Frazier, too, had great style when he dressed. In fact, his choice of fashion was one of the reasons he acquired his nickname. He had a variety of double and triple-breasted suits, expensive shoes, and often wore a wide-brimmed hat. Sometimes his duds looked as if they came from an earlier time, the 1920s or 1930s. That and the fact that he was such a ball thief on the court led a Knicks trainer to first call him Clyde, after the notorious Clyde Barrow, a 1930s bank robber whose life was chronicled in the film, *Bonnie and Clyde.*

Unlike Barnett, Frazier loved going to hot spots around Manhattan, but unlike Namath he often went alone. "I like to go out and meet people, at random, and just travel alone," he said. If he was at a gathering or a party and didn't feel there was a reason to stay, he'd suddenly disappear and turn up somewhere else. But when the team was on the road he often just stayed in his room, more or less isolated. "I can stay in my room all day and never be bored," he once said, adding that he could relax with music, television, or simply rest up for the next game. He had a strong sense of himself and loved the image he was building in New York and around the NBA. But he also made his personal preferences clear when he said, "I don't hang out with anybody on the team."

DeBusschere was the blue-collar worker, the family man, a guy who loved to guzzle a few beers in the locker room right after the game. He already had a wife and family to go home to after games at the Garden and had come to hate life on the road. As he put it, "I'm bored to death with [traveling], because I'm simply sick and tired of it. I always hope there's a cowboy movie on TV. That always kills a couple of hours." Life wasn't as glamorous as it sounded for many professional athletes. Sure, guys could always go out and find a good time. There were women, groupies, in every city, even back then. But for guys like DeBusschere it was just a matter of marking time until the next game and waiting for the chance to go home to his family.

Bradley was different. He lived the life befitting a graduate of Oxford and future United States senator. In other words, he had a variety of interests and friends and was always involved with activities far from the realm of basketball, though his priorities were never skewed, and during the season the Knicks always came first. DeBusschere, who roomed with Bradley on the road, said the phone rarely stopped ringing, and the calls were always for his roomie. Oddly enough, Bradley felt he played even better when he had a variety of things to occupy his time.

"On days when I've had 11 hours sleep, taken the proper number of limbering steps, eaten the right food, I don't think there's an obvious improvement [in my game]. [With] some of [my] best games, I've had no sleep, five appointments, worked in an office all day, and walked around the city too much."

Bradley was very disciplined in his activities, very organized, and simply felt he had to be productive in other areas. And, of course, he never stopped learning, always reading and studying something, whether it be a novel or an economic report. Needless to say, he also did not hang with his teammates much of the time. Many of his friends were away from the game. He was also the worst dresser on the team, wearing a rumpled trench coat a la Peter Falk in the TV series *Columbo,* and often wearing jackets and ties that had food stains or other blemishes on them. In an era when dressing sharp had become the mark of many athletes, Bill Bradley simply didn't care.

Cazzie Russell was a physical fitness fanatic, always looking for a place to work out and talking to his teammates about eating right, vitamins, and other healthful endeavors, to the point where it annoyed some. But Cazzie was Cazzie and simply did it his way.

Willis Reed was the captain and took his role seriously. In fact, much of his life was rooted in responsibility, from the time he hauled hay and picked cotton as a youngster in rural Louisiana. He had been the team captain at Grambling, often giving his team pep talks before the coach had a chance to say his piece. With the Knicks, Reed also played the role as liaison between players and coach, which sometimes made fraternization tricky. He often had to go to Holzman to discuss any complaints the players might have and, conversely, the coach would let Reed hear it when he wasn't happy with the team's effort during practice or a game. It was often frustrating for Reed, because Holzman also let the captain know that as the coach, he would always have the last word.

Reed also had to deal with the press more so than the other players, giving him yet another responsibility. But Willis was always about hard work, leading, getting up for the big games, and taking his job as captain very seriously. For all those reasons, he would never be in a position to embarrass himself or the team.

THE RACIAL SITUATION, CIRCA 1969

It was a very different world back in 1969. The top tickets to see the Knicks at the Garden went for $12.60, and the players got a whopping $16 per day meal money on the road. The state of the country and the world wasn't very good, either. The Vietnam War, which had polarized much of the country, was still raging. The assassinations of Robert F. Kennedy and Martin Luther King the year before began to make many feel that no one was safe anymore. King's death also ignited racial unrest and some rioting in a number of major American cities. Sports was an outlet, and the championships won by the Jets and then the Mets had really given the city of New York a much-needed shot in the arm, a very happy—almost euphoric—escape from the problems of the real world.

Major professional sports had been integrated for two decades. Jackie Robinson was the most celebrated pioneer, becoming the first African-American to play major league baseball when he joined the Brooklyn Dodgers in 1947. It was way too long in coming. When the modern NBA began as the BAA in 1946, there were no African-American players. Then in 1950, Chuck Cooper joined the Boston Celtics and Nat "Sweetwater" Clifton became a member of the Knicks. Within a few short years, many more African-Americans began coming into the league, many of them stars. By 1969, you would think that there would be no more problems, just teamwork. But as mentioned before, individuals don't have to like each other to play well together. When you have a relatively small group of people together so much, individual tastes, backgrounds, and cultures will sometimes clash. And the Knicks, being a microcosm of almost any diverse group, were not without problems.

It was not that unusual on most teams for black and white players to go their separate ways after games. But so will two white players or two black players who happen to have diverse interests and lifestyles. There were, however, sensitivities to the overall racial situation in the country. As Dick Barnett said, "After you leave the arena, you're just another brother out there, just like anybody else." He also was not surprised that the black and white players on the team were not close friends. "There are so many forces [at work]," he explained. "You have the environmental forces, you have the forces of culture, so many different things."

For example, all the players didn't like the same music, and some would complain about the volume when a style of music they didn't care for was turned up. There was also some sniping during the year about the coach not treating all his players the same, complaints that had some racial overtones to them. At the same time, some players simply did not like each other, and if one happened to be white and the other black, well, the problem tended to be magnified. Bill Bradley spoke of the situation with the eye of a sociologist rather than a basketball player.

"I imagine it's difficult for any black person in the racist society we live in to be sure of a white man's motives," he told a writer, "whether he is real or phony, whether he's sincere or deceiving. As a result, specific unconscious actions on the part of whites are often interpreted as racial actions by blacks. Once you peel away all the layers of experience, that's what's there."

The same situation undoubtedly existed in many others kinds of workplaces where people were thrown together in close proximity for long periods of time. It never became a huge issue and, as mentioned, the players often went their separate ways off the court. And, fortunately, there was never an issue that affected the team on the floor. The relationships between the players were simply part and parcel of the times, of players coming from different backgrounds, cultures, and even different parts of the country. When you have that, there will always be differences and some conflicts.

A LONG-STANDING RECORD IS TIED

Now it was back to business. With the team at 18-1 and already off to the best start in NBA history, fans began to wonder if this well-oiled Knicks team would ever lose. No one could win them all, but with the exception of that early-season blemish against Golden State, the Knicks were doing a pretty good impression of the perfect team.

They traveled to Philly and won a close one, 98-94 against the 76ers, then topped the Suns at the Garden, 128-114 to make it 20-1 and run the win streak to 15. A 103-96 win over the

Lakers followed, then an easy, 138-108 victory over the Hawks at Atlanta that not only brought the team's record to 22-1, but allowed the Knicks to tie the record of 17 straight wins by Washington and Boston.

The Atlanta game gave fans another glimpse of the explosive power of the Knicks, and it was usually initiated by the team's great defense. The game was actually close in the first half, already high scoring, as the Knicks held just a 68-61 advantage. Then, in the second half, the essence of the team was never more in evidence. The Knicks began to both intercept passes and steal the ball in a way that made a good Hawks team look as if it was playing in a high school league.

It started with a DeBusschere interception, which turned into a pair of successful free throws by Frazier. Then Barnett picked up an errant pass and turned it into a quick bucket. Next Bradley swiped the ball from the hands of Lou Hudson and tossed it to Clyde for another hoop. Seconds later, Bradley was at it again, pilfering the ball from guard Walt Hazzard and again finding Frazier for another lay-up. Then the fast hands of the wily and predatory Clyde took center stage. He swiped the ball from Hazzard three straight times and helped convert each into another New York basket. In a matter of minutes, a close game had become a rout.

The final score was 138-108, a game in which the Knicks completely dismantled a very proficient veteran NBA team. Their defense had made the Hawks look like a group of rank amateurs, kids playing against men, and the ease with which the New Yorkers broke it open must have opened even more eyes among NBA followers, especially those who never took the Madison Square Garden habitants seriously. This team looked as close to unbeatable as any, at least during this magnificent run they were making to open the season. Walt Frazier had finished the game with an incredible 15 steals. Bradley had put the clamps on Hudson, one of the league's top scorers. Frazier did more than shine on defense. At the other end, his improving offensive game resulted in 33 points, a total matched by the always-efficient Reed.

Now there was a day off before the Knicks would attempt to make history. They were trying to stay low key about it, playing them one game at a time, but they had to be aware that a victory over the Cincinnati Royals on a neutral court in Cleveland, would allow them to do something no NBA team had ever done before—win 18 straight basketball games.

THE COOZ STANDS IN THE WAY

The Cincinnati Royals were no longer a major NBA threat. The team had peaked in the mid-1960s but was now on the downside, a sub-.500 organization. Cincy was still led by the great Oscar Robertson, but some felt the Big O was not only tired of losing, but beginning lose a bit of his own magic touch. What made it worse this season was that the team had shipped star center Jerry Lucas to Golden State at the start of the season. Lucas was one of the game's best rebounders and a good scorer. That pretty much doomed Cincy to a less than mediocre season. Tom Van Arsdale, the twin brother of Dick, was a solid player, but after that the team really didn't have much firepower.

Nevertheless, there was some unexpected interest in the Royals. Former Celtics great Bob Cousy had taken over the team's coaching reins at the beginning of the season. One of the game's legendary players, Cousy was a star during the first phase of the Celtics dynasty and still considered one of the great guards in league history. Of course, great players don't always make great coaches, but a week before the big game with the Knicks, Cousy announced he was activating himself, returning to the court seven years after playing his final game in Boston. Apparently, Cooz felt he could light a fire under his team by showing them how he wanted it done. And what better way to do that than to put his shorts and sneakers on and take to the court once more? How much Cousy could contribute to the outcome of a game as a player was anybody's guess.

The way the Knicks had played in Atlanta two nights earlier, most felt they would eat the Royals for dinner. But the ball often has a strange way of bouncing, and this one was a struggle from the start. The team wasn't sharp. Maybe they were a bit worn down by the schedule or the pressure of going for the record. They were also playing their sixth game in ten days, three at home and three on the road. The NBA shuttle can be exhausting at times, and almost every team runs out of gas now and then. Only the Knicks didn't want it to be on this night at the unfamiliar Cleveland Arena.

Cincy came out as if they were the team going for the record, while the usually active Knicks seemed to have their shoes glued to the floor, or at least leaden with weights. At the end of one, the Royals had a 30-23 lead. The New Yorkers needed a lift and got it in the second quarter from Cazzie Russell. The hot-shooting sixth man came in and did his thing, hitting on six of seven field goal tries and a pair of free throws, his 14 points helping the Knicks gain a 55-52 halftime advantage. Fans looked for them to turn it on again in the second half, as they had against Atlanta, but this time it didn't happen. The Royals continued to play well, and the lead changed hands several times in what looked increasingly like a game that would go down to the wire.

THE FINAL SECONDS

With just 1:49 left and the Royals leading by three, 101-98, the Knicks caught a break. Oscar Robertson fouled out. With the Big O gone, everyone looked to the Cincy bench to see which player would take his place. Suddenly, the arena erupted when

The floor leadership provided by Frazier was instrumental in the Knicks early-season, 18-game win streak. AP/WWP

Bob Cousy took his warmups off. The coach was putting himself in a very big game at a very big moment. It was almost as if the arena was suddenly enveloped in a time warp as Cousy, his hair already graying, came out on the court. The Cooz certainly didn't look like the player who had once dazzled the NBA with his ball-handling and passing prowess.

Yet suddenly Cousy began playing as if were fully prepared to turn back the clock, working the magic he had shown to Boston fans all those years. He started out by whipping a crosscourt hook pass to Norm Van Lier, who hit an open jumper. Minutes later he was fouled and without hesitation sank both shots from the charity stripe. A Knick hoop in between, and the score was 105-100, Cincy in front, with just 26 seconds to play. It looked as if the streak was about to end, and in a very unceremonious way in a strange arena against an inferior team that was being led by a graying, 41-year-old player/coach.

With time running out, Barnett brought the ball down, stutter-stepped and shook Cousy, bringing a pair of other defenders toward him. That allowed Reed to free himself near the hoop. Barnett hit him with a quick pass, but the captain missed the shot. Undaunted, he grabbed his own rebound, and when he went up again he was fouled by Van Arsdale. Because the Royals were over the foul limit, Reed was allowed three shots—the old three-to-make-two rule—and made a pair, bringing the score to 105-102. Cincy then called timeout when they couldn't make the inbounds pass. That gave them the ball at midcourt, and Cousy finally made a mistake. His inbounds pass intended for Van Arsdale was picked off by DeBusschere, who raced to the basket and dunked the ball home. That made it 105-104 with just six seconds left.

Cousy again threw the ball to Van Arsdale, who began dribbling up the right sideline with DeBusschere guarding him. If they fouled him and he hit the shots, the game would be over. But then Mike Riordan, who had come in for Barnett at the timeout, raced over to double-team the dribbler. Van Arsdale tried to change direction without changing hands, and Reed, who had also drifted over, deflected the ball in the air just as Van Arsdale tried to pass. There was Walt Frazier, Clyde-on-the-spot, grabbing it and heading back the other way with two seconds left. He saw DeBusschere underneath but didn't know if there was enough time to pass the ball and then have Dave go for the lay-up. Instead, Clyde launched a mid-air one-hander that clunked the back rim but came right back to him as he leaped toward the hoop. He tried to shoot while still in the air, and Van Arsdale fouled him with virtually no time left. Two shots.

Frazier, who was not the world's best from the foul line, now had the game and the record sitting squarely on his shoulders. Make them both, and the team wins. Make one, it goes to overtime. Miss both, and the streak is over. He stepped to the line as the 10,438 fans in the old arena screamed and waved their arms in an effort to distract him. Frazier took a deep breath, and calmly swished the first free throw. Then he stepped back, came up again, took another breath, and won the game with the second shot, 106-105, a record 18th straight victory!

"When I got my rebound and tried to put it back up on the way down, I was wishing like hell that it had gone in," Frazier would say. "I didn't want to go to the line like that. At times I stand on the line like I'm standing in mud. My feet, no matter how I put them, don't feel comfortable. If I had missed the first one, I would have been a little uptight. But when I made it, I knew it was over."

The celebration lasted long. Maybe it wasn't so much the record, but the way the team had found a way to win a game that seemed all but lost. To be 23-1 after 24 games, covering almost a third of the season, was remarkable. The Knicks had made a statement, let the rest of the NBA know they were not only for real, but determined to ride on top all the way to the end. It was almost as if they were now declaring themselves the new kingpins and daring the rest of the league to knock them off the mountain.

But they wouldn't have long to celebrate. They had to return to New York immediately for a game the next night against the Pistons.

CHAPTER 5

INJURIES AND THE SCHEDULE BEGINS CATCHING UP

THUD! THE STREAK ENDS

Though they still hadn't won a thing, hadn't duplicated what the Jets had done in January or the Mets in October, the Knicks were already the toast of the town. While the two championships brought to the city in football and baseball were met with euphoria and ticker-tape parades, there still seemed to be something special about the Knicks. Football players, save a Joe Namath and a few select others, are often couched in anonymity, their faces covered by a helmets and facemasks, their bodies bloated by shoulder pads, hip pads, thigh pads. In their uniforms, they almost didn't look human. The large roster precludes the fans really knowing all the players, save the obvious stars. Much of the same is true with baseball. Sure, when the Mets won, many of the players were treated as real heroes, but there was still a 25-man roster, and fans tend to focus their attention once again on just the few big stars.

With the Knicks, it was different. Because basketball is played in a more intimate setting with just a 12-man roster, it's not difficult for the fans to see the entire team up close and personal. Even the uniform allows the fans to really see the players, check out their expressions and hear them communicating on the court. There is also more television and radio exposure for everyone because there are fewer players, almost giving fans the feeling of being on a first-name basis with them. Fans simply loved the makeup of this Knicks team, and after a 23-1 start and record-breaking win streak, it was as if they could do no wrong. Many felt the team had a real shot at breaking the NBA's all-time best record, the 68-13 mark set just three years earlier by Wilt Chamberlain and the Philadelphia 76ers. The record notwithstanding, the Knicks were already the obvious odds-on favorites to succeed the Celtics as NBA champs.

But nothing lasts forever. When the Knicks were introduced to another sellout crowd at the Garden that November 29, the fans stood and cheered, the ovation lasting nearly five minutes. The players, in turn, waved to crowd in what could be described as an early-season love-in. The visiting Pistons players watched quietly, then took to the court determined not to become victim number 19. They came out like gangbusters, scoring the first six point of the game while the Knicks still seemed to be recovering from the aftermath of their emotional victory over the Royals. The team looked tired and flat.

Slowly the Knicks came out of it, not wanting to just mail it in on a night they knew they were less than at their best. The lead continued changing hands during the first three quarters, then with just less than 10 minutes remaining, the Pistons began to take control of the game. This time there would be no emotional, last-minute comeback. The legs just weren't there, and their shooting had gone cold. Dave Stallworth, expected to provide some instant scoring along with Cazzie Russell, didn't get a single point in 13 minutes of play. Mike Riordan, now firmly entrenched as the third guard, had only a pair in 15 minutes of action. When the buzzer mercifully sounded, the mediocre Pistons had beaten the Knicks, 110-98, ending the winning streak and giving the Knicks just their second loss of the season.

The players knew it was bound to happen, so none of them appeared overly deflated by the defeat. This wasn't going to be an 81-1 team when the season ended. And maybe, with the pressure of the streak gone, they could simply concentrate on winning basketball games, one at a time now. As Willis Reed said after the game, "This only proves we're human."

A COUPLE OF KEY MATCHUPS

Most of the Knicks were philosophical about the end of the streak. It had to happen sooner or later was the company line. Even the usually acerbic Holzman, who usually found a problem with the team under every rock, shook this one off without threatening a rough practice the next day. The prevailing attitude was that it had to happen, the streak had to end, as every streak ultimately does. Now the players were ready to concentrate on the rest of the season. That's exactly what the Knicks seemed to do when they went out and topped Seattle, Baltimore, and Milwaukee, winning by margins of 20, 9, and then 25 points. With an incredible 26-2 record, it appeared that even the streak-ending loss to Detroit hadn't affected or deterred the team at all.

Both the Baltimore and Milwaukee games were a kind of barometer. These were the two teams chasing the Knicks in the East and, in the eyes of some, the next best teams in the league. The Western Division was a tossup. Atlanta had the edge at this point, but had already been proven no threat to the Knicks, and the Lakers without Chamberlain just weren't the same team. For L.A. to challenge, the big guy would have to make it back for the playoffs. Baltimore, on the other hand, had a group of talented individuals and an unselfish center in Wes Unseld. When they had it all together, they could run and gun with anyone. The Bucks, in just their second year, were riding on the back of the rookie center Alcindor and beginning to win a lot of games. So once again, even at this point in the season, the Knicks felt they had something to prove.

The matchups with Baltimore were especially intriguing. Frazier was on Earl Monroe. The "Pearl" was a dynamic scorer with no end to his juking, spinning moves that usually freed him from most defenders. He was always a real challenge for Clyde. Barnett had Kevin Loughery, who didn't have the natural talent of Monroe, but a guy who worked hard and could flick his jumper in the wink of an eye. Bradley was always matched against the 6'7" Jack Marin, a lefty scorer who could get under your skin because he talked a lot on the court. He and Dollar Bill had more than one shoving match during the season. DeBusschere was matched up against powerful Gus Johnson. Gus could jump and score, but the hard-working DeBusschere usually played him to a standoff. Burly Wes Unseld might have only been 6'8", but like Reed he was strong and hard to move. A great rebounder, he also had the ability to throw that quick outlet pass to start the fast break. The Bullets had one of the highest scoring teams in the league, and that made them still another challenge for the defensive unit of the Knicks.

It didn't help that this game was being played at the Baltimore Civic Center. Good teams can win anywhere, but in the NBA the cheering crowds and friendly confines of a home arena usually constitute yet another sixth man. The only change this night was that Loughery was out of the lineup with an injury, and Mike Davis started in his place. Davis hit a quick jumper off the opening tip, and the Bullets got the start they wanted. They continued to pour it on, and at the end of the first quarter the Bullets were up by 21 points. The Knicks hadn't trailed by more than 12 all year, and suddenly they found themselves on the wrong end of a blowout. Lesser teams might have folded it up right then and there. But not these New Yorkers.

In the second quarter, the Knicks began fighting back, and it was the guys off the bench who started the turnaround. Cazzie got hot, hitting four of five shots. Stallworth and Riordan helped, too, bringing some speed to the lineup and running with the quicker Bullets. Then Reed, who Holzman was going to pull in favor of Nate Bowman, got mad when he perceived some rougher-than-usual treatments from a couple of his opponents. That inspired the captain to go on a tear of his own. He began dominating Unseld inside and led another furious scoring barrage that put the Knicks up by six at halftime. It was a huge turnaround, but the game wasn't over yet.

In the third quarter the Knicks "D" took over. Frazier went on one of his defensive tears and put the clamps on the Pearl. He also intercepted a couple of Unseld outlet passes that led directly to Knicks baskets. A 15-2 New York run put the game out of reach, and the Knicks coasted home with a 116-107 victory. Even more impressive was the fact that the team continued unbeaten on the road, winning all 12 games thus far. Now they headed for Milwaukee and a meeting with Alcindor and the Bucks.

Milwaukee was a first-year expansion team in 1968-1969 and did surprisingly well, finishing last but with a less-than-abysmal 27-55. Then they drafted Lew Alcindor. The 7'2" center out of UCLA was in the process of living up to all his advance notices. With a supporting cast of virtual no-names—Flynn Robinson, Jon McGlocklin, Bob Dandridge, Greg Smith—but guys who could play, nevertheless, Alcindor had transformed the team into a winner. The rookie center was near the top of the league in scoring and rebounding, and was already proving a force. But the Knicks weren't worried.

Maybe that was because Willis Reed had absolutely no fear of the big guy. Reed always looked back at a preseason meeting with the Bucks, his first direct clash with the rookie who was making all the headlines. "I knew that night I'd always be able to handle him," the captain said later. "He was light and easy to move out of the paint."

Reed and the Knicks proved it on this night, winning easily, 124-99, as Frazier and Bradley scored 29 points apiece. So they headed back home with a 26-2 record, tying the 1966-1967 Philadelphia team for the fastest start ever. That was the club that finished at 68-13, and many felt the Knicks were going to easily top that mark. The club was playing well, was supremely confident, and seemed to match up favorably every team in the league.

A SUDDENLY BUMPY ROAD

The one-night homecoming started as another love-in as the Garden crowd greeted their returning heroes who had been out of town for seven days. It ended with a 103-101 loss to the Cincinnati Royals, leaving everyone with a kind of empty feeling. This was the kind of team that should never beat the Knicks, not these Knicks. Then it was back on the road where they beat the Bucks again, returning to Milwaukee just five days after their last meeting. This time they won by a single point, 96-95, but 24 hours later, playing in Seattle, the Knicks were beaten, 112-105. Back home, the 76ers defeated them, then the Atlanta Hawks, a team they handled with ease the last time and almost embarrassed with their ball-hawking defense, topped them in a shootout, 125-124. What happened to defense? And how in the world did this team, that had won 26 of its first 28 games, suddenly lose three straight?

For one thing, the little bumps and bruises that accompany the long NBA season were beginning to pile up. The indispensable Reed had an injured toe and a bad stomach that began to hinder his effectiveness, Clyde had a groin pull,

DeBusschere had been hit in the mouth and experienced some light-headedness. The team came back from the three losses with three victories, including a Christmas night win over Detroit. Then it was off to an immediate cross-country flight for a game the next night at Los Angeles, which the obviously tired and jet-lagged team lost. From there, the team had to make a jaunt up to Vancouver, British Columbia, the next night for a neutral court game against Seattle. They won that one, went back to Phoenix the next night and won again, then came back to the Garden to beat the Bulls two nights later.

This Christmas-week itinerary that began with the flight from New York to L.A. and wound up back in New York to host Chicago was a four-night odyssey that covered nearly 7,200 miles. Who in the world made that schedule? There wasn't much time to rest, just running to and from airports, suiting up, playing a game, and trying to remember which city was next. A loss at Milwaukee, 118-105, on a night when Reed obviously didn't handle Alcindor all that well, gave the Knicks a 33-8 mark at the halfway point of the season. It was still a great record, and they were still in first place. But was this really the same team with the same kind of killer instinct and total effectiveness that started the season at 23-1? That was a question beginning to prey on a lot of minds.

SOME FINGER-POINTING BEGINS

The second half of the season began with a 111-104 loss to the Celtics. It was only the second time the Knicks had played Boston and to lose at the Garden was almost embarrassing. These were no longer the invincible Celts of Bill Russell and a team headed for its first losing record since 1949-1950. John Havlicek was the only Celtics star now, and replacing Russell at center was someone named Henry Finkel. And still the Knicks lost, something that would have been virtually impossible earlier in the year.

It was the brutally honest Barnett who came out and said, "Even when we were winning, there were still guys that didn't like each other. I was listening to Carl Eller...when the Minnesota Vikings won the championship [and] and he was giving his bullshit about everybody loves each other. What did he say [the next year] when they lost? When you're winning, everything is great, everybody loves each other, and everybody is a great guy."

Obviously, with the team going just 10-8 since their winning streak ended, all was not well in Knickerbocker land. This certainly wasn't the same team that was blowing everyone out the first six weeks of the season. The minor injuries didn't help, and the offense had turned it down a notch, the players just not as sharp on the shooting end. A couple of the guys on the end of the bench also noticed that the levels of complaints were rising.

"A lot of guys are beginning to criticize each other," one player said. "Everyone on the bench is doing it when they come out of the games, and even some of the starters are doing it. I can't understand why it is [that way] and it kind of irks me a bit...It just makes me feel insecure."

Holzman, of course, was known as a defensive coach, and many of the players felt he concentrated so hard on the "D" that he forgot about the offense. Much of what the Knicks did on the offensive end, according to one player, came from another source.

"Most of our offense is from DeBusschere," the player said. "He put in all the good plays. We didn't have any of this stuff we have until he came last year."

There was also more noticeable sniping between coach and players during games, and that good feeling from a month earlier seemed to be disappearing. Now players were finding fault everywhere—with each other, with the travel schedule, and with the accommodations in some of the other cities. If they didn't put it all behind them and start playing ball again, a potentially great season could suddenly come apart at the seams.

ANOTHER LONG ROAD TRIP

From January 6 to 18, the Knicks had seven straight road games, including one on a neutral court in Salt Lake City. Being on another of those airport-hopping adventures wasn't the best thing for team morale, especially at a crucial part of the season. Ironically, the team would begin to win again, taking five of the seven games, losing only at San Diego and then at Boston. The trip started with a big, 30-point victory at Baltimore, something that should have indicated that the Knicks as a team were back. Then they won a pair at San Francisco, playing the Warriors twice in three nights, but the sniping between players was continuing. Then the team traveled down to San Diego to play the three-year-old Rockets, led by their 6'9" forward, Elvin Hayes.

The Rockets were in last place, and beyond Hayes they didn't have much. But on this night they had more than enough to beat the Knicks, 123-115. Holzman was irate that his team could lose to the Rockets, and, as usual, he voiced his dissatisfactions with the captain. Reed's stomach was apparently bothering him, and at half time the coach carped that Willis wasn't getting back fast enough on defense. An angry Reed sat out the second half, one of the reasons for the relatively easy San Diego win.

NOT THE TROTTERS

A neutral court game against Phoenix at Salt Lake City, Utah, was another source of annoyance for some. This time the reason was the preliminary game, the highly entertaining Harlem

Globetrotters against their usual patsies, the Washington Generals. The Trotters, of course, were one of the first all African-American basketball teams, started by a man named Abe Saperstein way back in 1927. That was in the sport's early barnstorming days, and the Trotters played serious basketball back then, their only counterparts being another all-black team, New York Renaissance. Back then, the Trotters (and the Rens) were good enough to beat other pro teams and proved it many times in those early years whenever games could be arranged.

Now, however, the Trotters were a comedy act. They still had skilled players, but their sole object was to entertain, and they had a number of set routines they went through each game that left fans, especially kids, laughing and enjoying themselves. In the early days of the NBA, they were often part of doubleheaders to spur attendance. By 1970 they pretty much traveled on their own but were still occasionally paired with an NBA game to bring in the fans, especially when the game was being played in a city that didn't have a regular NBA team. That was the case in Salt Lake City, but it didn't sit well with some of the Knicks who felt the Trotters brand of ball didn't belong as part of a serious night of competitive basketball.

Dave DeBusschere was one who wasn't particularly happy. "I'm not mad at the people for laughing," he said. "Just say I'm mad at being billed with the Trotters, because I get sick and tired of being asked, 'Do you think if you guys played the Trotters you could beat them?' Heck, they have some guys playing for them that couldn't even make NBA expansion clubs."

AND THEN THERE WAS CONNIE HAWKINS

There was still another reason for DeBusschere being so testy that night. The Phoenix Suns were led by 6'8" forward Connie Hawkins, who was playing his first year in the NBA at the age of

There are always bumps and bruises during the long NBA season. Despite having to wear a guard to protect a nose injury, Dave DeBusschere continued to compete at a high level. AP/WWP

27. Hawkins had been a New York City playground legend who went off to the University of Iowa in 1961. But he never played a single game because of a basketball point-shaving scandal that broke back in New York. Hawkins, it was suggested, allegedly introduced some players to gamblers who were fixing games. Iowa bid him a quick adieu, and the NBA said he would never play a game in one of their uniforms. Yet Hawkins was never convicted of any wrongdoing, and years later a magazine article said he was really innocent, just a scared kid who agreed with investigators when they made some veiled suggestions as to his role in the whole sordid affair. He finally sued the NBA and was allowed to join Phoenix in 1969.

Why did Hawkins's presence irk DeBusschere? It was a matter of pride. For one thing, when the two teams met early in the season, the Knicks won easily, but Hawkins had torched the Knicks for 27 points and sent DeBusschere to the bench early with foul trouble. After that game, Double D praised the late-blooming rookie, saying, "He's got the biggest hands I've ever seen. He handles the ball like a baseball and he doesn't run, he just floats or sort of glides."

But that was then, this was now. When a local Phoenix reporter passed on a remark that Hawkins was the better player, DeBusschere began to burn. Hawkins, indeed, was special, one of the first players to go one on one making several moves while soaring through the air. He was almost Julius Irving before there was a Doctor J, a totally different kind of player than DeBusschere. But on this night DeBusschere was still chafing about the Globetrotters and about the newsman's remark when he took the court. Playing with concentration and intensity, as well as with uncharacteristic physicality, he shut down Hawkins, and the Knicks won, 130-114. What did it matter if the campers weren't always happy as long as the team won?

CAZZIE GETS MIFFED IN DETROIT

The next game was in Detroit, but the team didn't stay in the Motor City. It wasn't like it is today, where professional athletes get the red-carpet, first-class treatment wherever they go. The $16 daily meal money should confirm that. For the game in Detroit the ballclub stayed north of the border in Windsor, Ontario, in Canada. By then, with the sixth of the seven road games looming, the team was really tired. The day of the game, which was scheduled for that night, Cazzie Russell was driving back from Ann Arbor after visiting friends from college days. That's when it happened.

His car was pulled over by the police. When Cazzie got out, one officer approached him while the other stood behind the hood of the patrol car with his revolver trained right at the basketball star. It was a tense couple of minutes, and had Cazzie made a wrong move, he might well have been shot. As it turned out, it was a case of pure mistaken identity. The police were looking for an African-American prisoner who had killed a deputy and escaped while being transferred to another facility. It was said that he resembled Cazzie. The phrase "racial profiling" wasn't used back in those days, but a case certainly could have been made for it, and the incident unnerved Cazzie.

He was angry all day and into the game. He almost came to blows with a teammate and had words with his captain. Reed finally told him to save his anger for the game and Cazzie responded, scoring the key hoops in the closing minutes as the Knicks won a close one, 104-102. Two nights later the road trip ended with a 109-102 loss at Boston. Even without Bill Russell, the Celts were proving a hard nut for the New Yorkers to crack.

THE SHIP APPEARS RIGHTED

A five-day break helped revive the ballclub, and then one more road game took place in Chicago before the Knicks returned home. They beat the Bulls, 120-117, the first game in what would be the beginning of a nine-game winning streak, taking the team from 38-11 to 47-11, and putting the New Yorkers back on the track to produce one of the best NBA seasons ever. The streak included a couple of wins over Boston, getting that monkey off their backs. But looking with the critical eye, most of the games were against sub-.500 teams. No matter. A win is a win.

The most lopsided victory in the streak came on January 27, at the Garden against the Celtics. In this one, the Knicks had it going at both ends and wound up winning, 133-100, humbling the once-great franchise that had won their 11th title just a year earlier. In that game, however, Bill Bradley suddenly came up limping. The result would be a torn medial ligament in his ankle, but not knowing that at first, Dollar Bill carried on. He played just two minutes the next game against Detroit, but by the time the club played the Bulls two games later, he was back full time and scoring 19 points. All told, he played eight games after hurting the ankle, though at less than full speed much of time, resulting in more court action for Russell and Stallworth. The win streak ended on February 4, when the team had one of those unexplainable nights and was beaten by the Atlanta Hawks, 111-96. After they won back-to-back games against the Royals, running their record to 49-12, Bradley decided to shut it down.

The Knicks' team physician had been ill, and a full diagnosis wasn't made immediately. By playing and favoring his injured left ankle, Bradley also strained his back. Finally, a specialist looked at the ankle, and that's when the usually super-active forward finally decided to sit out. So just when the well-oiled Knicks machine seemed to be functioning on all cylinders once again, one of the main parts had been sent out for repair.

CHAPTER 6

HERE COME THE BUCKS AND BULLETS

WITH BRADLEY ON THE SHELF

Bradley stayed in his West Side apartment for a week between February 7 and 14. Most of the time he remained in bed, elevating his foot and putting virtually no weight on his ankle. The Knicks would play 14 games without their starting forward and go 9-5. For most teams that wasn't bad. But in the preceding 19 games before Bradley went on the shelf, the team had been 16-3, their best streak since the dominating start. So there's little doubt the chemistry of the club had been altered.

Restored to a starting role, Cazzie Russell seemed to flourish. The first four games, in which he was on the court for the opening tip, resulted in 24-, 35-, 19-, and 18-point performances. To the casual fan, it might have appeared that the Knicks had more offensive firepower with the hot-shooting Russell on the court. Cazzie's 35-point performance came in a 151-106 crushing of the 76ers, Philly's worst defeat ever, and the

Knicks' second best scoring output in franchise history. So everyone was putting the ball in the hole that night.

But to show the fragile psyche of the professional athlete, Russell's scoring outburst made Bill Bradley almost come back to reclaim his spot early. Only the cautionary words of Dave DeBusschere made Bradley realize it was best for him and for the team to let his ankle heal fully before returning. After all, while these games counted, it was the playoffs that everyone was already pointing for.

WHAT ABOUT BRADLEY VS. RUSSELL?

There was no doubt that both Bill Bradley and Cazzie Russell were outstanding basketball players. That had been obvious back in their All-America college days. Both excelled and brought their teams along with them on a winning ride. Though both players were the same height, Russell was more of a physical specimen, yet using his strength wasn't the focal point of his game, though he was probably a little bit better rebounder than Bradley. Not surprisingly, Dollar Bill was the better passer and garnered more assists.

Russell also had a habit that annoyed Holzman no end. He went after rebounds with one hand, preferring to snag the ball then snap his other hand onto it. It might have been a flashy maneuver in the eyes of some, but there were those singular occasions when the one hand resulted in the ball skittering away, and Holzman would holler from the bench for Cazzie to get two hands on the ball. But Cazzie seemed to love the flash and dash, just the way he loved it when one low-trajectory jumper after another found the bottom of the net.

The purists knew the right answer. Both players had game, but Russell's would have been better designed for a running team like the Bullets, or a rebuilding/expansion ballclub that needed a star, a guy expected to pile up the points. When he did this for the Knicks in five and 10-minute spurts, he was contributing in a positive way. In that sense, he was an integral part of the team.

But when New York was firing on all five cylinders, when the team was dismantling opponents as they had at the outset of the season and during the recent winning streak, the total team game played by Bill Bradley was the better fit. He was part of the Reed-Frazier-DeBusschere-Barnett-Bradley combination that played as one, that did all the little things as a team that allowed them to dominate at both ends of the floor. In the final analysis, it was apparent that this version of the Knicks was a better team with Bradley in the starting lineup and Russell coming off the bench.

First Place Not Yet a Lock

Despite the incredible start and the NBA's best record for the entire season, the Knicks still weren't a lock to finish first. When they finished the first half of the season with a 33-8 record, the young Milwaukee Bucks were hanging around at 27-14, and the Bullets were just a game or so behind them. No one thought that the Bucks, in just their second year, would be a factor, but the presence of Lew Alcindor had made them a surprise contender.

As mentioned, the players behind Alcindor were pretty much no names, but they had game. Guard Flynn Robinson was the second-leading scorer capable of throwing in 20 a game. Jon McGlocklin, a 6'5" guard, who attended Indiana with the Van Arsdale twins, also played a lot like them. He averaged nearly 18 a game and was called by some, "the third twin." Young forwards Bob Dandridge and Greg Smith both hustled and could rebound despite not being overly big. Dandridge averaged around 13 a game and Smith 10. When Alcindor's nearly 29 points a game was added to the mix, the Bucks' starters were a dangerous group. They also had some useful reserves in rebounding forward Don

Smith, former All-Star guard Guy Rodgers, and veterans Fred Crawford and Len Chappell, both ex-Knicks.

But the big guy was the main man. As the season wore on he was becoming more confident and more active. His skyhook was quickly becoming the single most unstoppable shot in the game, and he had surprisingly good range on it. While Willis Reed had said early on that he would have no trouble handling the rookie because of his superior strength, he soon found he'd have to work very hard to keep his prophecy intact.

In a January 2 game at Milwaukee, which marked the halfway point in the season, the Bucks gave the New Yorkers a glimpse of the future, and it wasn't pretty. For the first time, Alcindor wasn't allowing Reed to push him around. He was getting used to the rough play in the NBA and learning how to compensate. Plus, he was tougher than he looked. He was also a good six inches taller than the Knicks captain, so when he got the ball down low he could shoot over Reed with relative ease. On this night he was hot. Though he would adopt the Muslim name of Kareem Abdul-Jabbar the following season, on this night Lew Alcindor was unstoppable. He scored 24 points in the first half, ran his total to 41 after intermission, and the Bucks beat the Knicks for the first time, 118-105.

Willis scored just 16 that night, and somewhere in the backs of the players' minds a little bell must have been ringing. *If we have to face these guys in the playoffs, it's not going to be a cakewalk.*

As For the Bullets

The Knicks and Bullets were bitter rivals, and it had been that way ever since DeBusschere's arrival the season before. Baltimore might have played a run-and-gun, helter-skelter type of game, but they were good. Though the Knicks handled them for the most part, they were making life very difficult for other teams around the league, and they matched up very well against New York. The Knicks really had to be on their team game, with the defense working overtime, to keep the Bullets at bay.

When the two teams met, the matchups were almost classics. Frazier and Earl Monroe were both becoming huge stars, yet played a completely opposite game. Reed and Wes Unseld were similar in size and strength, though Reed was more of a scorer while Unseld was a ferocious rebounder and threw great outlet passes. Gus Johnson and DeBusschere pitted strength against strength. DeBusschere had the edge stopping his man on defense, but Johnson gave his club a second 1,000-plus rebounder. Both scored at about the same clip with Johnson having a small edge because of his team's run-and-gun tactics. Jack Marin, who averaged close to 20 a game, was a better scorer and rebounder than Bradley, but Dollar Bill was the superior passer and played a great, all-around team game. Kevin Loughery averaged nearly 22 points a game, second to Monroe, and about six points more than Barnett, but Dick had the advantage on defense and was a streak shooter capable of getting very hot.

The Knicks probably had the slight advantage with Russell, Riordan, and Stallworth off the bench, but these were two very evenly matched teams. More so, there was no love lost between them. Up to this point, the Knicks had handled the Bullets pretty easily. Baltimore would win just one regular-season game against the New Yorkers, but in the playoffs, anything could happen.

THE NEW YORK-BALTIMORE CONNECTION

There was yet something else that made the Knicks-Bullets rivalry even more intense. The City of Baltimore had been taking a rather humiliating beating from the big city to the north. First it was the Jets. The 1968 American Football League champs led by quarterback Joe Namath had defeated a heavily favored Baltimore Colts team, 16-7, the previous January in what would become known as Super Bowl III. What made it more humiliating was the fact that the Jets were the first AFL team to ever beat a National Football League team in the championship game. The two leagues would complete a full merger in 1970, but the loss hit the prideful city hard. The Colts has been number one with the fans ever since quarterback John Unitas led them to a pair of NFL titles in 1958 and 1959, both over the New York Giants. Johnny U was hurt in the Super Bowl, and by the time he got in, it was too late.

Next it was time for baseball and the Mets. The New Yorkers were an expansion team back in 1962 and soon the laughingstock of the National League. But in 1969, led by Manager Gil Hodges and two great starting pitchers—Tom Seaver and Jerry Koosman—the team caught fire, won 100 games and the National League pennant. They did that by sweeping the Atlanta Braves three straight in the first ever division playoff. Waiting for them in the World Series were the Baltimore Orioles. Like the Colts, the Orioles were heavily favored. They were a great team, led by colorful manager Earl Weaver, Frank and Brooks Robinson, Boog Powell, Paul Blair, and a great pitching staff. What happened? The Mets came out and beat them in five games to become champions.

So now Baltimore fans looked to the Bullets. They loved the team and felt it had the potential to go all the way. Should the Bullets end up meeting the Knicks in the playoffs, whatever happened before would go by the boards. It would be all-out war.

THE WEAKENED WEST

For a good part of the season, only the Atlanta Hawks were playing above .500 in the NBA's Western Division. Led by guard

Lou Hudson and forwards Joe Caldwell and Bill Bridges, this was a good, but not great Hawks team. Late in the season the team made a trade for, of all people, center Walt Bellamy. But his presence didn't unnerve the Knicks. They knew enough about Big Bells from New York days and felt they could handle the Hawks with no problem.

The Warriors were another team that some expected to make a run. But once center Nate Thurmond went down with a broken leg early in the second half of the season, the Warriors' hopes plummeted. Chicago, Phoenix, Seattle, and San Diego simply didn't have enough firepower to threaten any of the top Eastern teams. The only wild card in the equation was the Lakers.

When the team played in Minneapolis in the early days of the NBA, they were something of a dynasty. Led by 6'10" center George Mikan, basketball's first great big man, the Lakers won five titles in six years. Then Mikan retired and the team went into eclipse. The franchise moved to Los Angeles in 1960, and by that time had a pair of superstars in Elgin Baylor and Jerry West. As good as they were, they could never get past the Celtics, losing to the Celts six times in the Finals and becoming the ultimate bridesmaids. The last loss came the season before, in 1968-1969, which turned out to be Bill Russell and the Celtics' swan song. That defeat also came with Wilt Chamberlain in the lineup, and the team still hoped Wilt could help put them over the top.

Then came the big guy's knee injury early in the season and with him went the Lakers' hopes. Now, however, there were signs that Wilt might return for the playoffs. If he did and was in reasonably good playing shape, L.A. might surprise. So all three of the top Eastern teams were keeping a close eye on the happenings out west and listening for reports of the big center's rehab. Wilt, with his immense talent, could become the wild card once the playoffs began.

THE PUBLIC AND PRIVATE KNICKS

It was almost the dawn of a new era when it came to relations between the press and professional sports teams. In the early days of baseball, for instance, reporters traveled by train with the teams, wrote about the games and little else. They were often personal friends of the players, drinking with them and playing cards, and never would violate what was termed the sanctity of the locker room. In other words, there was very little written about the personal lives of the athletes and almost never anything negative. Unless someone made the police blotter, where it couldn't be hidden, there was no reporting of problems between players or players and managers.

One of the first books ever written about professional sports that violated the so-called sanctity of the locker room was *Ball Four*, written by Jim Bouton, who had pitched for the New York Yankees from 1962 until he was traded in 1968. Two years later his book was published with much fanfare and criticism. Bouton had actually dared to tell not-so-flattering stories about Yankees icons such as Mickey Mantle, and his best-selling tome signaled the beginning of a no-holds-barred kind of journalism that would spread to the daily beat writers, as well. The change was already beginning during the 1969-1970 season and sometimes made the Knicks uptight.

For instance, the general public didn't know anything about conflicts between player and coach, player and player. They didn't know that there were sometimes differences between the black and white players, where the culture and lifestyle of one could annoy the other. There was not much known when players carped about getting more playing time. And the few stories that leaked out from time to time angered coach and player alike.

DeBusschere, for example, had a longstanding habit of downing a few beers after a game. One day a picture appeared in a sports magazine showing him in the midst of a big swig. Knicks management quickly told the photographer not to take that kind of photo again. Even Double D agreed it was not a good thing to show the general public, not a good thing for his young admirers to see.

Members of the daily press who traveled with the team were treated better, as a rule, than the freelancers, writers from various magazines and publications sent to do a single story about the team. And because of the way the Knicks were playing all year, there were many. These guys were looked upon with more suspicion since they didn't get the "perks" given the daily press. They would write their stories and be gone, so management figured there was more chance of getting a dose of reality from them, in effect, a "chop" job.

Many of the daily writers tended to hang out with Holzman and other team officials, and thus tended to give him much of the credit for the team's success. That often irked the players. Others complained when writers tried to portray the Knicks as the picture-perfect team. But many fans wanted to see it that way. The Knicks were *their* team and they didn't want to read about disharmony, racial antagonism, backbiting, and individual egos at play. Those few in the know hoped the team would hold it together down the stretch and regain the full magic of the early season.

Of course, today's media is different. Every team is fodder for a feeding frenzy, and the press tries to outdo itself—uncover the dissension, break a scandal, follow the players around town to see what they did in their spare time. In that respect, the Knicks had it easy. Many players and teams of recent vintage have had to deal with a lot worse.

A COUPLE OF LOSSES
CAN MAKE YOU THINK

It wasn't so much that the Knicks were 9-5 while Bradley rested his ankle. Some might have considered that a slide, but they had won nearly two games for every one loss. As a rule, you won't find a team that can't live with that. Only there were a couple of losses during that stretch that merit a second look, because they were the kind of games the Knicks simply wouldn't have played earlier in the season. For example, a February 21, game with the Hawks resulted in the Knicks' worst defeat of the season, 122-106. This was a team the Knicks had handled easily most of the year. Where was that great Holzman "D"?

Then there was the 110-104 loss to the Bullets. Everyone knew how good the Bullets were, but the Knicks seemed to match up so well with them, the proof of the pudding being that the New Yorkers had won ten straight. Until now. Then there was a 133-116 loss to the Sixers, a team the Knicks had scored 151 points against just three weeks earlier. Sure, this was a time when teams regularly scored over 100 points, sometimes way over, but not normally against a Knicks team that regularly held teams under 100. Then in the final game before Bradley's return, played on a neutral court in Portland, Oregon, the Knicks lost to the Seattle Supersonics, 115-103. The loss was significant for two reasons. One, they shouldn't have been beaten by a recent expansion team on the way to a 36-46 record. And two, had they won, the Knicks would have clinched the division title.

Now that would have to wait. But with Bradley due back and the next game against San Diego, they would have a chance to wrap with all five starters in action. They had better. There were just seven regular-season games left.

WOULD WILT BE BACK?

There was another piece of news that began trickling down at the beginning of March. It said that Wilt Chamberlain was getting closer and could indeed be back for the playoffs. Some doubted it, citing the kind of surgery Wilt had undergone shortly after the beginning of the season. That usually put guys on the shelf until the following year. But Wilt was no ordinary mortal. The big guy wasn't just a basketball superstar, he was a physical marvel. At 7'1" and now close to 290 pounds, Wilt was not only fast and agile, but also reputed to be the strongest man in the league by far. And that was saying something considering the power in players like Willis and Wes Unseld, as well as a number of others. On the court, however, Wilt didn't always play with the kind of ferocity that others did. Some said that if he were as mean as he was strong, the entire NBA would get out of his way.

But would he be back? The Lakers were giving mixed signals. Their team physician, Dr. Robert Kerlan, had said several times that Wilt was probably through for the year. Even when the Lakers said Wilt would soon begin practicing with the team, the doctor was skeptical, saying there was little chance that Wilt's knee could have healed enough for him to withstand the rigors of NBA play. One Knick who felt all along that Wilt would be back was Willis Reed. The captain had seen enough of Wilt over the years to know there was no way he would miss a chance at another title. Willis went on record saying that if the Lakers went deep into the playoffs, Wilt would be on the court.

THE CLINCHER

Tempers had flared again during the loss to Seattle. The team wasn't in sync, wasn't executing the way a team approaching the

The celebration was low key after the Knicks clinched the division title. As captain Willis Reed shows, the team was number one, but the all-important playoffs still loomed ahead. AP/WWP

eve of the playoffs should. Frazier became annoyed at Dave Stallworth's tendency to go one on one and ignore the team concept and let him know it when he returned to the bench. The TV cameras caught it and beamed it back to New York. DeBusschere quickly rushed over and diffused the potential confrontation. Just 24 hours later the team was in San Diego with Bradley ready for some court time, his first in almost five weeks. And once again, a victory would give them the Eastern Division title.

The Knicks took the early lead but in the second quarter the Rockets began closing the gap. Elvin Hayes, as usual, was hitting a variety of medium-range jumpers and working the boards. At the same time, Cazzie was having trouble defending the streak shooting Jim Barnett. Finally, Holzman couldn't wait any longer and put Bill Bradley in the game. Dollar Bill played just four minutes his first time back on the court. He didn't score, but right away some of the little things that had been missing returned. He hit Clyde with a nifty bounce pass that led to a layup, and the defense tightened up immediately.

With just the brief lift that Bradley gave them, the Knicks regained control and rolled to a 119-113 victory. They now had a 59-17 record, still the best in the league, and more importantly, they had clinched the division crown. The celebration was relatively mild, no spewing of champagne, no noisy reporters grabbing every player they could find. As Bill Bradley put it, "The feeling was, 'So we clinched it.' I didn't feel anything. I don't think anyone else wanted a big celebration."

In a sense, it was quiet and dignified. Maybe one reason was that the team knew the upcoming battles would be tougher than anything they had faced so far. The Bucks and Bullets had come on strong in the second half. Before the Knicks could look to the West and maybe find out for certain whether Chamberlain would be back, they would have to get through their own division. That, they knew now, wouldn't be easy.

CHAPTER 7

GETTING READY FOR THE PLAYOFFS

PLUSSES AND MINUSES

With six games left in the regular season, the Knicks were Eastern Division champs. In the NBA, however, that doesn't mean much, not in the long run. Look what happened the season before. Baltimore won the East with a 57-25 mark, followed by Philadelphia and the Knicks, three games separating the three teams. The Celtics, aging rapidly, were fourth with a 48-34 mark, nine games behind Baltimore. In baseball, before the beginning of divisional play and the wild card, nine games out of first would put you on another planet. But in the NBA, it still qualified you for the playoffs. So first place meant little, even less when the Bullets were swept by the Knicks in the first round. First place, yes. Out of the playoffs, even faster.

When it all ended, it was the fourth-place Celtics again standing on top of the basketball world and getting tons of praise heaped upon them for turning back the clock and dominating the post season, as they had done so often. So finishing might have fostered some sense of accomplishment, but it wasn't really a reason to celebrate. It's who's cutting down the nets at the end that counts. The playoffs, or the second season as it's often called, are really what separates the men from the boys. If you can't win that four-of-seven series, then first, second, third place means nothing. The 12 most important victories must be accomplished in the second season, a sobering fact that tempered any premature celebration for finishing first.

Then what did the team do after clinching? They promptly went out and lost five of their last six games, including the final four in succession. That's not the optimum way to put the wrap on a season. Among the losses were a 106-101 defeat at L.A., a 116-108 beating by the Bucks at the Garden, a 136-120 pasting from the Royals, and a season ending 115-112 loss at Boston. Maybe they were playing out the string, but losing to the Lakers and Bucks, teams they could meet in the playoffs, wasn't sending a very good message. And if you do the numbers, the 60-22 final ledger meant that the Knicks were 37-21 after their 23-1 start, still good but far from great, especially after their totally dominating start.

With that in mind, they knew they were not a lock to win in the playoffs.

SOME REGULAR-SEASON NUMBERS

For a team that was running away with the entire league after the first seven weeks of the season, the Knicks had come back to earth. Their 60-22 final record enabled them to finish just four games ahead of the improving 56-26 Bucks. Lew Alcindor, the obvious Rookie of the Year, had certainly made his presence felt, finishing second in scoring behind Jerry West with a 28.8 average and third in rebounding behind Elvin Hayes and Wes Unseld. The Bullets were third at 50-32, ten games behind the Knicks.

The Hawks won the West at 48-34, with the Lakers next at 46-36. All the other Western Division teams were below the .500 mark. Atlanta was simply not considered a serious contender, and the Lakers, if they were to make a run, needed Wilt Chamberlain.

Reed and Frazier were one-two on the club in scoring, averaging 21.7 and 20.9 points per game, respectively. Reed had been doing that his entire career, but Frazier had now emerged as a full-fledged star with a complete game. Barnett (14.9), DeBusschere (14.6), and Bradley (14.5) showed balanced scoring from the starters. Russell was next with 11.5 points a game, mostly off the bench. Reed was also sixth in the league in rebounding with 13.9 caroms a game. DeBusschere was next on the club, grabbing 10 boards a game. Frazier, with everything else, was second to Lenny Wilkens in assists with 8.2 per game, and was also ninth in field-goal percentage, hitting 51.8 percent of his shots from the field.

Not surprisingly, both Reed and Frazier were on the first all-NBA team, joined by Billy Cunningham of Philly, Connie Hawkins of Phoenix, and Jerry West of the Lakers. It was at the all-important defensive end of the floor where the Knicks really made their mark. Reed, Frazier, and DeBusschere were members of the All-Defensive first team, joined by Gus Johnson of the Bullets and West once more. So it was obvious that the philosophy brought by Holzman had paid off. To have three members of one team on the All-Defensive club was quite an accomplishment.

But while numbers and honors are nice, it is wins that really count. So everything that happened in those first 82 games was now history. Looming on the horizon was the first round of the playoffs. The Knicks would have their hands full. On tap for the first round was the Bullets, and while the Knicks had pretty much dominated them in the regular season, everyone knew that this club would not go easily in the playoffs. They not only had pride as individuals and as a team, but were representing a city that had been taking it on the chin from New York (Jets, Mets) for the last year and a half.

The other series would feature the Bucks and the fourth-place 76ers. Milwaukee, with Alcindor, would be the heavy favorites. If the Knicks battled their way past the Bullets, they would then likely meet the Bucks for the Eastern Division crown and a trip to the Finals.

LIFE AT THE GARDEN

The success of the Knicks had done something else during this amazing year. It made Madison Square Garden the place to be and made tickets for the game in demand everywhere. It was where the so-called beautiful people wanted to be seen. In 1969-1970 it was chic to be a Knickerbockers fan. Celebrities from all walks of life were suddenly showing up at the games. No more kids in jeans and T-shirts. The Garden crowd was spiffed up, coiffed in finery that resembled some of the duds worn by the players.

The word sellout became commonplace as the attendance was almost automatic every time the team took the floor. It was 19,500, but sometimes it seemed as if even more people crowded into the newest incarnation of the Mecca of Basketball. To some, the new arena lacked some of the character and ambience of the old Garden, which seemed to sweat along with the players and was usually enshrouded in thick cigar smoke by the third quarter. But this was still a great place from which to watch, and the scalpers had a field day outside the arena every time the teams played.

It wasn't always that way. In fact, before the trade that brought Dave DeBusschere to the team, the place was usually about half full of only the most diehard of fans. Years earlier the old Garden was teeming with fans when college doubleheaders became the craze. Back then, it also brought out the gamblers that led directly to several rounds of college basketball scandals through the years. There was still plenty of gambling and nights when the fans were cheering as much for the point spread as the final outcome of the game. But there was little doubt that they loved their Knicks and dearly wanted that elusive NBA championship.

There were, however, some great stories from the earlier days of the Garden, many coming from longtime PA announcer John Condon. Condon recalled, for example, a rather boisterous female fan who would always attend games with her husband, who watched quietly in direct opposition to her always-flapping mouth.

"[One night] she was raising hell and the man sat there with his arms crossed the whole game, didn't utter a sound," Condon said. "When the game was over, his wife got up to go, straightened herself out and then turned to him. She gave him a tap on the shoulder and he toppled…Doctors estimated he had been dead since the first quarter."

Condon also knew that there was usually heavy gambling on the games, so he played around with the way he announced the scores of other games. There were times when he would give the winner first, but other times when he'd announce the losing team's score first. It drove the bettors crazy. He said he always knew when there was big money being bet. When he would begin to announce a certain score, the place would suddenly become so quiet you could hear a pin drop. He would sometimes get a kick out of pausing between the two scores, also driving some fans nuts. Finally, during one of these prolonged pauses and when the Garden was very quiet a leather-lunged fans shouted,

"What are you, some goddamn wise son of a bitch?"

The old Garden definitely had more characters and very vocal fans. There was a fat guy who would do all kinds of crazy dances during timeouts, and many courtside fans who knew the players by name would hold short conversations with them during the course of the action. A longtime New York Rangers fan recalled that when the Garden was converted over for hockey, the fans would get there early, turn their seats up to show they were taken, then go back outside and across the street for something to eat. No one would take the seats. During intermissions between periods, these same fans would go out into the hallways and play kick hockey with rolled up beer and soda cups. It was simply a fun time for real, diehard sports fans.

Now it was more corporate, more suits and ties, and more of the privileged people taking the seats. But the enthusiasm for the Knicks was never higher, and now with playoff fever gripping the entire city, the fervor for the hometown heroes was higher than ever.

MORE PRE-PLAYOFF WORRIES

The Knicks didn't just have the Bullets to worry about as the first round of the playoffs approached. Whenever they played Baltimore it was almost always a case of team vs. one on one. In other words, the Bullets like to run and gun, freelance, go one on one, and had the players to do it. The Knicks stopped them by playing great team defense, double-teaming when necessary, trying to keep the Bullets' best one-on-one players—Earl Monroe and Gus Johnson—under wraps with tight guarding from Frazier and DeBusschere. The trick was to keep from getting in a high-scoring shootout with Baltimore. But to do this, the Knicks had to be functioning at peak efficiency.

But would they? That was the question, since going into the playoffs there were still aches and pains, the kind of tweaks that wouldn't keep a player off the floor but might keep him from playing his kind of game. Let's check out the medical report.

There was no way, most thought, that Bradley could be in top shape. He had only played a handful of games since coming back from his ankle injury. So much of Dollar Bill's game was based on timing and movement, being in top condition. Even if the ankle was fully healed, there was a question of whether the former Princeton star could be in top game shape. If he wasn't, Holzman would have to spell him more often with Russell and/or Stallworth, and just a little bit of the all-important team chemistry would be lost. In addition, Frazier continued to complain periodically about his groin injury. It still bothered him, and if it escalated into a full-scale pull, the Knicks would be dead. No way they could win without Clyde operating at full strength.

And then there was the captain. Reed was the other indispensable cog in the wheel. Willis still had something of a balky knee. Though he was on the court full time right to the end of the season, some thought they noticed a difference in his play, especially in the final two games. He didn't seem to be jumping well. In fact, he wasn't really getting off the floor. The knee was examined very carefully by the team doctors. They said they found no structural damage and no calcium buildup. Yet it hurt. All the captain could do was work through the pain and maybe take a cortisone shot from time to time.

With Reed, fingers had to be crossed. It wasn't inconceivable that if the Knicks got by the Bullets, a series in which Willis would have to bump heads and bodies with the bulky, strong Wes Unseld, that he would next have to contend with the rookie Alcindor, whose game was improving by leaps, bounds, and skyhooks. And, if the team got past the Bucks into the final round, the Lakers might be waiting. And if they were, Wilt Chamberlain would be with them. The big guy had proclaimed himself fit for the playoffs, and even at less than 100 percent, Wilt was a force to be reckoned with. So the road wouldn't get any smoother, and the Knicks' captain, like the others, would have to endure.

A POSTAL STRIKE! NOT NOW

The minor injuries notwithstanding, it was almost beginning to look as if Lady Luck was not smiling on the Knicks. Two days before the playoffs were slated to begin, there was a nationwide postal strike. It wasn't that the team fretted about not getting all of its fan mail on time. The problem was that the National Guard was called up to help deliver the mail. Normally, that wouldn't mean much to a sports team, but back in the 1960s many athletes went into the Guard to fulfill their military obligation. On the Knicks were Private First Class Cazzie Russell and Private Michael Riordan.

Without warning they were deployed to man a post in one of the city's boroughs to help with mail delivery. Knicks officials almost had a collective stroke. What about practice? These were the first two guys off the bench and an integral part of Red Holzman's rotation. While the team was making phone call after phone call to try to get the two players back, Riordan was behind the wheel of a truck in Roslyn on Long Island, while Russell was working at an armory in the Bronx. The two missed a couple of practices but fortunately were back when the opening bell rang. Just another minor inconvenience.

NO CIRCUS THIS TIME

There was an unavoidable and painful truth facing Knicks fans. Their team was one of just three original franchises remaining that had played in the first NBA season of 1946-1947, and the only one that had never won the championship. The other two original teams were the Celtics and the Philadelphia Warriors. Philly had since moved to San Francisco, and the old Syracuse Nationals were now the Philadelphia 76ers, but the Warriors had won a title while still in Philly, and everyone knew how many the Celtics had won. This team, obviously, gave the franchise its best chance yet, and fans were hoping to see the early-season Knicks in the playoffs, not the flat and seemingly disinterested team that lost its final four regular-season games.

At least there was a more professional aspect to playoff basketball in New York now. Back in the 1950s when the Knicks did make the playoffs, they often found sawdust on the floor of Madison Square Garden instead of a basketball court. That's because the circus was in town and took precedence over everything else, including *professional* basketball. Now, finally, the NBA was big enough so that nonsense like that could not go on. A team played all of its home playoff games at home, no questions asked.

It was also a time when winning the NBA title had a greater financial prize, though nothing like it is today. When Red Holzman was a member of the champion Rochester Royals back in 1951, the total revenue the league received from the playoffs was in the $50,000 range. Of that, the players got precious little. Now the revenue was up around the $400,000 mark with close to $120,000 to be divided among the winning team.

In older times, money was always an incentive to winning the World Series, an NFL or NBA championship. Players' salaries were not high, and even if the winner's share was a mere $1,500, it made a player's life a lot easier. In 1970, the league was right on the edge of paying the players bigger money, as Bradley's $500,000, four-year contract attests. Today, of course, that contract would be chump change, and that's why today's players find the big, plushy championship ring the prize they want. The money, though very good, is incidental, because the salaries are through the roof. It's the bragging rights that come with wearing that ring that makes the modern player drool.

In 1970, it was a combination of both. At least the Knicks knew that no matter how deep they went into the playoffs, their home games would be at the Garden and they wouldn't be supplanted by a gaggle of elephants, trapeze artists, and clowns. They just wanted to be sure that they didn't end up being the clowns. If they lost after such a great season, they might as well leave town and join the circus themselves.

PLAN A AND PLAN B

Both the Knicks and the Bullets were practicing hard for a series each knew wouldn't be easy. It didn't matter that Baltimore had beaten the Knicks only once in the last ten tries, there was no sense of doom from the Pearl and his teammates. They knew they were good and knew that on the right night they could compete with anyone. As for the Knicks, they still felt as if they were the superior team, and in the long run their defense, controlled game, and team effort would prevail. It might not be in four or five, but it would happen.

During their final practices, the Knicks continued to work on the fundamentals of their defense, pressing and trapping, talking to each other and making sure that five guys were functioning as one. The team also knew it had to have a big effort from its stars. Frazier had to put the clamps on the Pearl, and DeBusschere had to nullify the high-flying offense of Gus Johnson, as well as playing him to a standoff on the boards. Everyone expected Reed to be his usual forceful self in big games. They knew his knee was hurting, but they also knew their captain. Once the bell sounded, Willis would give 100 percent from start to finish. He could handle Wes Unseld.

Center Nate Bowman didn't have Willis Reed's strength, but he gave the team some key minutes throughout the season. Photo by Vernon J. Biever

Plan B was unfolding in Baltimore. A Baltimore assistant coach and former NBA player, Bob Ferry, had scouted the Knicks extensively late in the season. He was often seen sitting in the stands at games taking copious notes on a clipboard. He was charting the Knicks plays, some of the sets the Knicks used every night. When they started running these plays in Game 1, the Bullets would be ready.

The agility of the modern player allowed more freelance in the game of the late 1960s. While teams had some set plays, they were always prepared to vary them, or to improvise at the last second. So it was difficult to completely nullify a team by knowing its offensive plays. You might stop them on one or two trips down the court, or maybe steal the ball or intercept a pass, but teams would adjust quickly—good teams, that is—and the chess match would start all over again.

It wasn't that way in the 1950s. NBA teams back then had favorite plays that they would run over and over again, and they did them so well, with so much precision, that it was difficult to stop. It was like the old Green Bay Packers sweep in the NFL. Vince Lombardi's team practiced this basic running play incessantly, and while opposing defenses knew it was coming, they more often than not couldn't stop it. The old St. Louis Hawks had a play in which forward Bob Pettit would get the ball behind a double screen and take his jump shot. As with the Packers, opponents knew it was coming, saw it being set up on the court, but if the Hawks did it quickly and smoothly, more often than not Pettit would be taking his jump shot from behind a double-screen, and the defense just had to watch and hope it didn't go in.

Everyone expected the Knicks/Bullets series to be fast-paced, rough, and always contested. The prevailing thought was that while the Knicks were favored, it was more likely to be a hard-fought tossup. Then, just before the series was to begin, the Bullets had another incentive. They, and the rest of the basketball world, learned that Willis Reed had been named the NBA's Most Valuable Player for the 1969-1970 season.

LET'S GET READY TO RUMBLE

The opening series was set to begin on March 26, at the Garden, and that made it the place to be in New York. Tickets officially topped out at $12.95 for a courtside seat back then which, like the price of gas, has gone out of sight since. Of course, the scalpers got much more, and there were plenty of people willing to pay. The diehard fans who had stuck with the team through thick and thin—certainly much more thin—now had to share seats with corporate types, women who were there just to be on the arms of their men, and some celebrities who became instant fans once these New Yorkers became the glamour team of the NBA.

There was a time when Ned Irish, the president of the Knicks and the guy who first put collegiate doubleheaders into the Garden, had to use all his professional guile, marketing and promotional skills, to get fans into the Mecca of basketball when the Knicks were in town. He tried to coax entire families to the Garden—dad, mom, and the kids—a night of entertainment. No such incentives were needed now. The old-school regulars who screamed and yelled in frustration through much of the 1950s and early-to-mid-1960s, didn't mind having the so-called new fans alongside them. Nothing mattered now but rooting for the home team and trying to help bring a first NBA title to New York.

The Knicks, of course, still had some small hurts. The condition of Reed's need wasn't really public knowledge at the time, so the biggest worry was over Bradley's ankle, and whether he'd be able to go full speed. The worst-case scenario was Bradley re-injuring the ankle and being forced out of the playoffs. For the

Bullets, guard Kevin Loughery would be playing with a five-pound aluminum and sponge vest to protect his healing ribs.

Earlier in the season Loughery had run into the rookie Alcindor and emerged with broken ribs and a punctured lung. He was good to go but might be hampered by the protective device. Third guard Mike Davis was already out with an injury, so rookie Fred "Mad Dog" Carter would be the backup.

Finally, it was time to do battle. The second season was about to begin, and with it the final quest for the Knicks. Could they duplicate what the Jets and Mets had done the season before, bring a championship to the city of New York, and a first for the Garden dwellers at the same time?

CHAPTER 8

A BATTLE AND AN UNEXPECTED BREEZE

THE PEARL

There had to be somewhat of an ominous feeling for Knicks fans when the Bullets took to the floor. Make no mistake, this was a very good basketball team. They had talent, youth, flair, and a penchant for putting on a great show. Nothing dull about these guys from Baltimore. They were physically strong, yet acrobatic, with the biggest offensive threat being the man called the Pearl.

Earl Monroe had learned his game on the schoolyards of Philadelphia before going on to Winston-Salem State, a Division II school where he averaged 41.5 points a game as a senior. He was a 20-point-plus scorer from his first day in the NBA and loved to put on a show for the fans. In the one game the Bullets had won from the Knicks during the regular season, Monroe had torched the New Yorkers and Walt Frazier for 37 points. If he could do that against the widely acknowledged best defensive

119

guard in the league, then he was certainly capable of leading his team to an upset.

Monroe's penchant for one-on-one play might have been diametrically opposed to the philosophy espoused by the Knicks, but for the Bullets his array of moves that usually resulted in a good shot were objects of adulation and sometimes awe. Monroe sometimes like to back into the man guarding him, showing him his rear while surveying the floor, looking to move left or right, spin, or turn and shoot while fading away. His guile also allowed him to break down the double-team and still find a good shot. He was Rookie of the Year in 1967-1968, then led the Bullets to the best record in the league the year after that.

The Knicks, however, had beaten the Bullets in four straight after Baltimore had finished first in the regular season. And now they were playing essentially the same team. But center Unseld was just a rookie then, albeit good enough to win both the Rookie of the Year and MVP Awards. Monroe was in his second season, and Gus Johnson was hurt. Now they were a year older, wiser, and healthier. The biggest difference, most felt, was the Pearl. During his first two years he was often one-dimensional. Once he made up his mind to shoot, that's what he did, regardless of circumstance. Now the Pearl also looked to pass, making him even more dangerous and the biggest threat to end the Knicks' season somewhere over the course of the next four to seven games.

GAME 1

In the opening minutes of the first game, Madison Square Garden was strangely quiet. Maybe the circus should have been in town, because it sure looked as if the Knicks weren't. The Pearl came out as if he owned the court, starting off by hitting his first jump shot. Then he picked off a Knicks outlet pass and went in for a lay-up. Next time down he scored on a nifty drive, going around a pair of New York defenders. Then Jack Marin faked Bradley out of his shoes and hit a jumper from the corner. Within minutes the Bullets were in command at 12-2. At the other end of the floor they were surprising the Knicks by calling out New York's offensive plays before they could develop and getting into position to stop them. A Barnett jumper from the corner stopped the bleeding, at least for the moment.

Holzman then wisely called a timeout so the Knicks could gather themselves and get it back together. There was no panic. The team had been in this position before, though not that often, and there was plenty of time left to right the ship. In fact, even in the days before the three-point field goal, an NBA team was more than capable of scoring points in bunches so that even an early 20-point lead was never really safe. Holzman told the Knicks to play their game, to SEE THE BALL and HIT THE OPEN MAN, the same kind of basic advice that had led to success all year. But, as always, the advice had to be augmented by execution. The timeout seemed to change the momentum and back on the court the Knicks began to click.

Barnett drove past the rookie Carter, who started in place of Kevin Loughery, for a lay-up. Then DeBusschere scored off a steal and Frazier hit a mid-range jumper. The Knicks came all the way back very quickly and within minutes had taken a 14-13 lead.

THE GAME BECOMES A BATTLE

Once the early runs were over, the two teams began going at it just the way everyone expected. There was a constant ebb and flow to the game, with momentum seeming to change every few minutes. If one team had the overall advantage, it appeared to be the Bullets, because they seemed to be imposing their will on the

Knicks, making the New Yorkers play more one on one then their usually controlled, defensive team game. During he regular season the Knicks let the NBA in defense, allowing just 105.9 points game. They won by an average of 9.1 points a game. Next best was Milwaukee, allowing 114.2 points a game and winning by 4.6 points an outing. The Lakers actually allowed 111.8 points but only won by a 1.9-point margin, because they didn't score as much. But the Knicks were far and away the top defensive team and won their games by the largest margin. Now, in the first game of the playoffs, the Bullets were matching them hoop for hoop.

The Pearl continued to plague the Knicks and finished the half in spectacular fashion, scoring six more points in the final two minutes while giving his team a 52-46 lead. In the third quarter, the Knicks defense finally came alive, with both Reed and DeBusschere flexing their muscle on defense and then also doing it on the offensive end. They combined for 25 points between them while doing a defensive job, especially on Johnson and Marin. The brought the crowd alive, and the chants of *"Dee-fense! Dee-fense! Dee-fense!"* rocked the Garden. Inspired, the Knicks finished the quarter with a slim lead.

A GREAT FINISH

Both teams continued battling throughout the second half, the outcome of the game in doubt. In any short series, the team winning the opener has a tremendous advantage, magnified even more if the visiting team can get the initial contest on their side of the ledger. Finally, with time running down, it was still very much up for grabs. At the beginning of the game and again just before the first half, this one became Earl Monroe against the Knicks. The Pearl kept getting the ball. Frazier and his teammates knew what he had in mind, but couldn't stop the shake and shimmy that the Pearl was throwing at them. He scored the Bullets' final eight points, his last hoop giving Baltimore a 101-100 lead with 1:30 left.

With the pressure on, the Knicks couldn't score, and finally, with 38 seconds left, Monroe had the ball again. This time Holzman didn't want to take any chances. A hoop would all but put the game on ice. Barnett quickly gave a foul, and Monroe made the shot to make it 102-100. The Knicks inbounded, and the first time Bradley got the ball he did an imitation of the Bill Bradley from Princeton days, driving the baseline and hitting the tying hoop. But the Bullets still had 23 seconds left to go for the win, and guess who had the basketball again?

Earl the Pearl was clearly playing for the last shot. He didn't want to give up the ball and evaded a double-team as Barnett tried to trap him. With the clock running down, he leaned into Frazier, then turned and shot from the rear of the key as he backed away. Finally, this time, he missed. Unbelievably, Monroe would say later that he thought the clock was ticking down to end the third quarter. Play had been so intense, demanding so much concentration, that the Pearl lost track of the quarter. That's why he looked almost lackadaisical on the final shot. He thought he had another 12 minutes to play. But now Game 1 was going to overtime.

OT was like so much of the rest of the game. Baltimore again took the lead, quickly building it up to six, but the Knicks fought back. Finally a Reed hoop brought it down to two. With time running down, Monroe had the ball again. This time he knew the situation exactly. He wanted to kill the clock. Frazier knew it, too. He realized he'd have to go after the ball. Once again Monroe worked the ball to the top of the key, his favorite place from which to operate. He knew the Knicks would have to foul him sooner or later. Barnett began moving toward the Pearl, perhaps causing him to take his eyes off Frazier for a split second. Clyde let his right go, and his timing was perfect. He slapped the ball in the direction of Barnett. Dick picked it up and went to the hoop. Fred Carter had no choice but to foul him. Barnett hit both clutch free throws and tied the game again, this time at 110-110.

With 23 seconds left, Monroe had it one more time. It was almost a repeat of the last possession. The Pearl was waiting up high to put a final move on, and once again Clyde went after the ball with the guile and moxie of a riverboat gambler. He poked it free, and once again Barnett was right there, grabbing it and going for the hoop. Barnett launched the shot, and Fred Carter went up high to get it. He deflected the ball at the last second. Barnett, the Knicks, and nearly everyone in the Garden thought Carter got it on the way down, which would make it goaltending. Game over. But referee Mendy Rudolph called it a legit block. A huge groan went up from the crowd. The Bullets breathed a sigh of relief. The game was going to a second overtime.

DOUBLE OT

Unbelievably, this opening game was going to a second overtime, another five minutes of action, yet another indication to all that this series was not going to be easy. The Bullets were ready for war and weren't going to roll over, despite their lack of success against the Knicks over the past year. The pattern the entire game, and in the first overtime, was Baltimore taking the quick lead and the Knicks having to catch them. About time to switch gears.

In the second OT, the Knicks got out fast. Riordan, DeBusschere, and Frazier scored quickly, and the Knicks were out in front, 117-112. The pressure was getting to everyone. At one point, Holzman looked down the bench and called out, "Mike, Mike," an indication for Riordan to get ready to go into the game. One problem. Riordan was already in. Holzman really wanted Bradley. That one got a few laughs in a decidedly tense situation.

Despite falling behind, Baltimore wouldn't quit. With the fans shouted for *"Dee-fense! Dee-fense! Dee-fense!"* the Knicks couldn't quite deliver. The Pearl scored, and then Fred Carter hit a shot and a free throw. Suddenly it was tied again at 117. The game was already exhausting, and no one wanted a third overtime. That would be too much to take. Not to worry. With time running down, the Knicks ran a play to free up Bradley behind Reed. Once again it was the Baltimore defense that kept the Knicks from executing. So Reed took the pass instead. Gus Johnson tried for the steal, missed, and gave Willis his chance. The captain hit a short hook to give the Knicks a 119-117 lead. There were 31 seconds left.

Once again the Pearl tried to tie it, but this time Frazier played almost perfect defense, and he had to force a shot. No good. The Knicks got the rebound, and the Bullets fouled DeBusschere. Dave hit the shot, making it 120-117, and time finally ran out on Baltimore. The Knicks had won a hard-fought, exciting game to take a 1-0 lead in the series. At the same time, the Bullets had sent them a message. Don't expect this to be easy, because we ain't done yet.

ON TO BALTIMORE

In a scheduling quirk, the Knicks and Baltimore were alternating home courts, so Game 2 would be at Baltimore. The reason must have been that the two cities were in close proximity. In the West, the Lakers and Phoenix Suns were playing the then-traditional two-two-one-one-one. So the Knicks had to fly right down the coast that night. They kept thinking about the game. Earl Monroe had scored 39, while Willis led the Knicks with 30. As great as the Pearl was, he had missed a couple of key shots that could have won it for his team. Maybe that would get into his head if the same situation arose.

The top tickets at the old Civic Center went for just $6.25, less than half the cost at the Garden. The crowd was different, too, more of a blue-collar, working-stiff group who were probably hooked more on the Colts than the Bullets. But they surely liked this team, liked the excitement they created, and, of course, they hated any ballclub from New York. The defeats suffered by their beloved Colts in Super Bowl III and the talented Orioles in the past World Series were still open wounds caused by those upstarts from the Big Apple. Now all they could hope for was a measure of revenge, and since the Bullets were the instrument that could provide it, they took the team to heart.

For three quarters it looked as if the fans would get what they wanted so badly. Though the Bullets had suffered a heartbreaking defeat in the opener, they seemed the more confident team. It was as if they fully realized that, hey, we can beat these guys. They're not *that* good. The Knicks somehow managed to hang close, but they were getting precious little offense from Bradley and Barnett, and even the usually reliable DeBusschere was being outhustled on the boards by Unseld and Johnson. Monroe was being Earl the Pearl again, and Baltimore had a 51-48 lead at halftime. When they upped it to 71-62 midway through the third quarter they seemed to have taken control of the game, and the fans at the Civic Center cheered their every move.

The Knicks were starting to bicker among themselves. At one point DeBusschere came out of the game, watched for a few minutes, and then began hollering to his teammates to start moving the ball. In the huddle some players carped about not getting enough help on defense. At that point they had all the earmarks of a team that was in the process of finding a way to lose. Then they got an unexpected lift from an unlikely source.

RIORDAN TO THE RESCUE

Mike Riordan entered the game late in the third quarter. A year earlier, Knicks fans might have groaned if Riordan appeared during a key moment in a big game. He was an unlikely rookie then, an unheralded guard out of Providence College who was drafted in the 12th round in 1967, but he didn't stick with the team until a year later, then was spotted in just 54 games, averaging just 2.3 points per contest. Riordan had played in the shadow of All-American Jimmy Walker at Providence, and even his coach, Joe Mullaney, didn't think he was NBA timbre.

"Mike loved basketball to the point that 40 minutes was too short a game for him," Mullaney said, looking back. "He was so hyped up, so energetic and aggressive, that it often interfered with his play."

That part was true. The 6'4" Riordan was a fireball who loved to work out, loved to practice, loved to play, and worked his tail off even if he was playing a pickup game at the local park. At Providence, his aggression resulted in too many fouls, and he often had to take a seat after committing five of them. The New York-born Riordan got his big chance when he was invited to work out with the returning Bill Bradley so the Knicks could assess how far Bradley had regressed while at Oxford. At that time he was working for a fire department in Queens, and he jumped at the chance to participate in the unexpected practice session. It was during these workouts that Riordan impressed the Knicks with his hustle and aggression and his willingness to mix it up with anyone. The team didn't want to lose him and had him play in the Eastern League to develop and refine his game in 1967-1968.

A year later he made the club but didn't play much. But in 1969-1970, his work ethic paid off, and he was the third guard

Hustling Mike Riordan became a valuable reserve throughout the title run and was especially tough in the playoffs against the Bullets. AP/WWP

behind Frazier and Barnett. As the season wore on, Coach Holzman had more and more confidence in the hustling Riordan and didn't hesitate to call upon him in any situation. And this situation in game two was crucial. Riordan scored two points before the quarter ended with the Bullets leading, 83-77. He remained in the game as the fourth quarter began.

Being Mike on the spot, he took the opening tap from Reed and raced in for a quick lay-up. The next time he had the ball, he blew past Monroe and hit a shot off the baseline to narrow the margin to 83-81. Not only did Riordan continue to score in the final session, he also put the clamps on the Pearl. Monroe had 18 points over the first three but would score on just a single free throw in the fourth, thanks to Mike Riordan's defense. Still the game came down to the final minutes.

The Knicks had the ball and a 103-99 lead with 1:20 remaining. Now they wanted to kill the clock, but they killed too much, and with the 24-second clock running down, Bradley had to heave one up and it banged off the side of the backboard. However, the Baltimore players didn't go after it, because they thought it was a 24-second violation since it didn't hit the rim. But the rules said it just had to touch either the rim or the backboard, and an alert Bradley got the rebound. Again the shot clock ran down, and again Bradley took a last-second shot. This time it was an air ball, but as Unseld went to get it, DeBusschere actually slammed the ball with his fists and Reed grabbed it. Later he would say, "I didn't slap it [with an open hand] because Unseld is so strong."

This time when the shot clock ran down, Reed didn't take any chances. He slammed the ball through the hoop for the last of his 27 points. A final free throw by Barnett gave the Knicks a 106-99 victory and what appeared to be a commanding 2-0 lead. The unsung hero was Mike Riordan. In addition to putting the clamps on Monroe, he had scored 11 of his 13 points in the final session. And that's the mark of a champion, when a player comes off the bench and gives the entire team a life.

It now appeared that the Knicks were fully in the driver's seat.

It's In the Bag, or Is It?

With a 2-0 lead and heading back to New York, the Knicks appeared to be in control of the series. They had taken the Bullets' best shots in both Games 1 and 2, and yet prevailed. In addition, both the players and New York fans who traveled to Baltimore for the second game noticed how Earl Monroe was putting ice packs on both knees every time he went to the bench for a breather. If the Pearl was hurting and wouldn't be at full strength, then the Bullets were history. Some even thought the Knicks would duplicate their sweep of the previous season or, worse case, would wrap in five or maybe six.

Nothing, in fact, seemed to be going right for the Bullets. The day after their second defeat, they found that their flight to New York had been canceled because of an air traffic controllers' strike. Now they had to charter a bus. But while the Knicks felt great because they had prevailed in the first two games in come-from-behind fashion, the Bullets were also feeling a lot better than expected. Because of the way they had played in the first two, they felt confident they could beat the Knicks, and they were not about to quit. In fact, the sluggish bus ride gave everyone a chance to talk, to begin psyching themselves up for Game 3, and by the time they hit the locker room to get ready, they were a loud, boisterous team that couldn't wait to take the court.

Kevin Loughery got it started. He began urging his teammates to play hard, repeating the phrase, "Be an animal. Be a goddamn animal," several times, and then hollering, "I'm tired of losing to these guys." Soon, the other players joined in, and by the time they took to the court, they were ready. The team not only came out ready to play, they came out in a dour and rough mood. They would play a physical game and get away with everything they could. Unseld and Johnson, the team's two musclemen, were taking no prisoners. And when Loughery took his restrictive flak jacket off at the end of the first quarter, it lifted the team even more. If their two-guard was willing to endure the pain by leaving his ribs unprotected, then everyone had to go all out.

The game was played on Easter Sunday, but the Knicks weren't celebrating. They were cold and sluggish, committing turnovers, not playing with the controlled fury that had enabled them to pull out the first two. This was a team that had won 18 straight early in the season, so they obviously weren't overconfident and willing to lose one since they already had two. It was just one of those nights. Reed stood helplessly by as Unseld grabbed rebound after rebound. Loughery, without the brace, would score 13 of his 17 points in the second half, and both Monroe and Marin would hit six of seven shots after intermission. The final was 127-113, with Unseld's 34 rebounds more than the entire Knicks team had garnered. The Bullets had broken through. After the game, a jubilant Loughery explained why he had removed his protective rib protector.

"I couldn't do a thing with that damned brace on," he said. "I couldn't shoot, and you get so damned sick and tired of the Knicks beating you. If we didn't win this one, there wouldn't be much breath left in us."

That was true. A 3-0 lead would be impossible. At 2-1, the momentum was teetering on the brink. If the Bullets could win Game 4, it would definitely swing to their side. And that's just what happened. Playing once again in Baltimore, the Bullets were still on a high, and the Knicks on a hangover. Unseld continued his strong-armed tactics and grabbed 24 rebounds. Marin and Johnson both played great defense up front, holding Bradley,

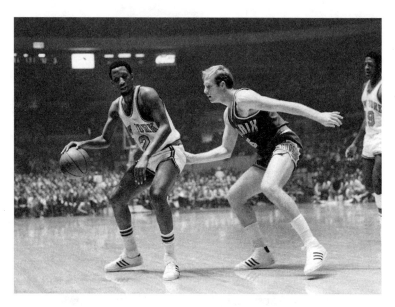

When Dick Barnett joined the Knicks, he had a reputation as a streak shooter. He turned out to be a lot more—a fine all-around player who excelled on defense and was dangerous in the clutch. AP/WWP

DeBusschere, Russell, and Stallworth to 13 for 43 from the field. Bad knees or not, Monroe was great again, and the Bullets won, 102-92. Now, it was down to a best-of-three series. No more euphoria in New York, because everyone knew that anything could happen.

ACHES, PAINS, AND PLAN B

With all the concern about Monroe's knee and his propitious use of ice packs, it was Willis Reed's knee that was suddenly the cause for concern. It had pained him all along, but by the fourth quarter of Game 4 it was beginning to hold him back. He couldn't jump well and that gave the bulky Unseld all the advantage he needed. It was a strange sight, watching Unseld operate, because no one—but no one—ever pushed Willis Reed around. The Knicks medical staff suggested another cortisone shot. At first, the captain balked. He knew that repeated cortisone shots could damage the tissue around his knee. His excuse was that he didn't want that long needle inserted into his knee. He kept the Knicks in limbo about whether he would take the shot or not.

At the same time Bill Bradley began using his Princeton, Oxford, and basketball brain. He began to see flaws in the way the Knicks were defending the Bullets and began to think about better ways to go about it. There was one problem. How would he broach his ideas to an old-school, I-am-the-boss coach like Holzman, and if he did, would the coach consider changing the game plan?

Much of the strategy was geared to stopping Monroe by having a more effective double-team when the Bullets cleared out one side of the court for their ultimate one-on-one player. Another change would be to keep Monroe busier on defense. The Pearl had been standing around outside the key, watching Barnett, but often edging downcourt early so he could take an outlet pass from Unseld. Bradley's plan was to have Barnett move through the lane more and go around the corners to occupy Monroe and keep him from being in prime position for the transition game. There was also a strategy to keep Unseld from coming out to the high post where he would take a pass, then dribble toward Marin and give him the ball while screening Bradley so the Baltimore forward to get an easy jump shot. There were things the Bullets were doing regularly in Games 3 and 4.

On offense, Bradley felt the Knicks should scrap the few plays that the Bullets were anticipating and handling successfully and rely more on those that would have Reed operating closer to the hoop. It was basic, not complex, and might be perceived by the observant fan as minor adjustments. But Bradley and the teammates he told agreed that they had to approach Holzman.

Then two things happened before Game 5. Bradley and several others discussed the changes with their coach and, surprise, Holzman gave them the go-ahead. And, just several hours before game time, Reed decided he would allow the doctor to give him the cortisone shot he abhorred.

THE PIVOTAL GAME

Before Game 5, Willis Reed called his teammates aside and tried to conjure up a sense of pride. "If the unity and closeness of this club is ever going to pay off, it's now," he said. "This is our moment of truth." What it also turned into was a throwback game. For the first time in the series, the Knicks looked like the team that had totally dominated the NBA over the first six weeks of the season. The cortisone shot did wonders for the captain. Reed was more active than in any previous game and was able to neutralize Unseld. Bradley hit his initial two shots of the game, and the first time the Bullets tried to isolate Monroe, Bradley rushed over for the double team, forcing the Pearl to hurry his shot and misfire. The little changes were working.

By the second half the Knicks looked fully like the fireball that had destroyed the NBA in the fall. For the first time in the series, the Bullets seemed to fall apart. The defense was so sharp, so precise, that no one on the Bullets could solve it, let alone get a good shot. Monroe and Gus Johnson were both frustrated. Marin wasn't getting those easy jumpers behind the Unseld screen, and there were absolutely no *gimmies*. The Bullets would hit only 10 of 59 shots in the second half. Reed, in the meantime, put on a show at both ends of the court. He had 36 points and 36 rebounds (remember all those missed shots) as the Knicks won easily, 101-80.

For the Bullets it was all futility. Johnson hit only one shot in 14 tries. Fred Carter was scoreless. The Pearl had a very un-Pearl-like 19 points, while Cazzie Russell complemented Reed by scoring 21 off the bench. With the 3-2 lead the Knicks could go back to Baltimore with a little more sense of comfort, but not too much. An explosive team like the Bullets could never be written off, despite what the successful change in strategy had produced in Game 5. There was still more basketball to play.

It Ain't Over Til It's Over

It's sometimes difficult to say what causes the flow and ebb in sports. How can a team be great one night and almost amateurish the next? What makes a group of players so sky high they're willing to run through a brick wall in one game, then play with a careless sluggishness the next? It's a dynamic that no one has successfully captured. If the answers were known, it would never happen. That's why when a team gets on a run as the Knicks did early in the season it's so special. And also very unusual.

Though Game 6 was played at the Civic Center, most fans expected the Knicks to clinch. So did the players, especially after the way the changes in strategy had paid off in the fifth game. In the first quarter, neither team looked as if it wanted to win. The Bullets made only four of 26 shots. That kind of shooting should have handed the game to the Knicks. But over the same period the New Yorkers hit on just seven of 23. Then Bradley and DeBusschere had to sit with foul trouble. Though the Knicks maintained a slim lead, Baltimore managed to stay close through the first half.

Finally, in the third quarter, the Bullets took control. Johnson and Monroe began to hit their shots while the Knicks continued to look asleep at the wheel. No comebacks this time. No last-minute heroics, just a slow countdown until it was official. There would be a seventh and deciding game. Baltimore won it, 96-87. The game couldn't have been more of a disaster for the Knicks.

Bradley hit just one of nine shots, DeBusschere two of 11, and the captain, who had been so sensational in Game 5, connected on only two of 14. For the Bullets, Monroe led the way again with 29 points, getting 19 of them in the second half. Johnson, too, erupted after intermission, canning 21 in the latter two quarters. The Knicks locker room was quiet. No passing blame, no clinical analysis. They had been awful and they knew it. The players talked almost in whispers, because they realized that they had not only let opportunity slip away, but had also put themselves in a position to lose. Should they come out flat in Game 7, or should Monroe and company have one of those nights where everything went in, then what was shaping up as the greatest season in Knicks' history would be over. Just like that.

GAME 7

Game 7. No need to explain what that means. You either do it or you don't. No second chances; no tomorrows, only an abject wait-til-next-year for the loser. And neither team wanted to utter those downtrodden words. Needless to say, the Garden was jumping for the biggest game the Knicks had played in years. The fans were ready to do their part. Down in the locker rooms, both teams were getting set. Reed's right knee was still sore, and he even made a painful utterance when trainer Danny Whelan touched it in the wrong spot. Generally the mood was somber, as it was for the Bullets. No one had to say anything. Motivational speeches were unnecessary. Both teams knew what was at stake. Even the usually vociferous Holzman had little to say. No SEE THE BALL! or HIT THE OPEN MAN! He had said that way too often already. Now he simply paced.

The crowd erupted when the Knicks came out, erupted when they were introduced, erupted several bars before the National Anthem ended. Then it was time to play. Holzman made one change before he sent his team onto the floor. He told Barnett to bring the ball upcourt, a job that usually went to Frazier. The coach wanted to keep Frazier as fresh as possible for his defensive work against Monroe. The strategy would work twofold. With his ballhandling duties diminished, Clyde could concentrate more on hawking the Pearl. And Barnett played as if he suddenly had a wake-up call. The wily vet was averaging just 12.5 points through the first six games, but he quickly found that when bringing the ball up he could get by Monroe, move into the driving lanes and either go to the hoop or pull up and launch that left-handed jump shot.

Led by the shooting of Barnett and great team defense, the Knicks once again looked very solid and took a 62-47 lead at the half. Then in the third quarter DeBusschere and Russell got hot. Not only did the hard-working forward do a defensive number on Johnson, he also found his shooting touch and scored 18 points over the final two sessions. And early in the third, the team got a huge lift from one of Cazzie Russell's patented hot streaks.

With the Knicks leading 68-53, Cazzie hit a jump shot, then at the other end blocked a jumper by Marin. Seconds later he put in a follow-up hoop, then hit another jumper. The Knicks not only had a 74-57 lead, but Cazzie's heroics jacked up both the bench and the crowd. Everyone could taste it. From there the Knicks almost cruised, coming home with a 127-114 victory to eliminate the Bullets. Finally. Barnett and DeBusschere had scored 28 points each, while Russell added 18. Frazier, in the meantime, had kept the Pearl in check, Reed played Unseld to a standoff, and with that kind of play, the Knicks almost always won.

When it was over, Garden organist Eddie Layton played "Happy Days Are Here Again," as the joyous crowd filed out. But those in the know didn't celebrate too much. They knew this was only step one. There was much more to come.

NEXT, THE TWO BIGGEST
GUYS IN THE LEAGUE

By the time the Knicks clinched against the Bullets on April 6, they already knew which team they would be playing in the next round. Three days earlier the Milwaukee Bucks and their rookie center, Lew Alcindor, had eliminated the Philadelphia 76ers in five games. The Bucks took the final three, including a 156-120 drubbing in Game 3 at Philly. There was no doubt now that this second-year expansion team was a real threat and that Alcindor could be on the verge of becoming the greatest offensive threat in the game. Milwaukee had also beaten the New Yorkers the last two times the teams met in the regular season. That in itself shortened the odds considerably.

There was something else the Knicks would have to think about. In the Western Division semifinals the Lakers had beaten the Phoenix Suns in seven hard-fought games. The big news in that series was the return of Wilt Chamberlain. The already legendary center had kept his promise to be ready for the playoffs. After L.A. won the opener, the Suns and Connie Hawkins took the next three, but in each game Wilt appeared to be getting stronger. Then the Lakers rallied, forcing a seventh game, and they blew the Suns out, 129-94. In the Western Finals they would be facing the Atlanta Hawks. With Wilt back, it was a foregone conclusion which team would win.

That meant that the Knicks, and especially their captain, could conceivably face the two biggest and arguably the best centers in the league. If Reed and the Knicks could get past the

Bucks, chances were pretty good that Wilt, Jerry West, and the rest of the Lakers would be waiting for them.

WITH SURPRISING EASE

Though Willis Reed had said as early as the preseason that he knew he would always be able to handle Lew Alcindor because of his superior strength, the rest of the league had slowly learned the trick was to put the clamps on the supporting cast. No one was going to stop Alcindor completely, but many of the young Bucks weren't battle tested and might have problems dealing with the increased physicality that always characterized the NBA playoffs. It was stern stuff, not for the faint of heart, and there were always epic playoff battles out on the court.

One of the keys was to hold down the team's second-leading scorer, guard Flynn Robinson. As one Milwaukee reporter wrote, "This is a complex, moody guy. He's more easily affected than most when things go wrong for him on the court…Flynn doesn't like hands on him on defense. …" Hand checking was common in the league then and tolerated by officials. Frazier, Barnett, and Riordan all knew what they would have to do when guarding Robinson. The only other scoring threat was guard Jon McGlocklin, but he was no Earl Monroe.

With this in mind, the Knicks won the first two games at the Garden, 110-102 and in a surprising nail-biter, 112-111. When somebody mentioned to the captain that he hadn't really been beating up on young Alcindor, who grew up in New York City, Willis just shrugged, "I don't muscle him," he explained. "I just keep him from moving in." In other words, Reed kept the young star from going where he wanted, dictating the position from which Alcindor would have to maneuver. As the youngster got more range on his great skyhook and more variety to his offense, no one would really stop him. For two decades he would go on as Kareem Abdul-Jabbar to become the NBA's all-time leading scorer and a five-time champion with the Los Angeles Lakers.

But let's not get ahead of ourselves. This series wasn't quite over. In the third game, rookie forward Bob Dandridge, normally no match for the physical play of DeBusschere, had it all going. Not only did he hit on 10 of 15 shots from the floor, but by keeping the Knicks' tough forward away from the boards, it gave Alcindor more room to operate. The big guy grabbed a career-best 31 rebounds and helped his team to a 101-96 victory. Knicks fans hoped this   wouldn't be a repeat of the Baltimore series and become another battle of attrition. But the Bucks were always

Willis Reed stood tall all season long, but never taller than in the playoffs when he had to go up against Lew Alcindor (33) and later Wilt Chamberlain. Even a severe leg injury couldn't stop him when the title was on the line.
AP/WWP

tough when Alcindor got help. Only the helpers couldn't do it every night, especially in the playoffs. Not yet, anyway.

ON TO THE FINALS

Part of the reason the young players couldn't put it all together was good, old-fashioned intimidation. The Knicks were a tough, battle-hardened team, and Willis Reed still had a reputation as one of the toughest guys in the league. His clean out of the Lakers his second year was still legendary. Typical of the effect Reed had on young players could be seen by something Milwaukee forward Greg Smith said after the second game in the series.

"I hit Reed in the mouth with my elbow as I came down with a rebound," Smith said, "and I apologized fast...as quick as I could get it out of my mouth. I'd almost hooked up with Reed in Milwaukee earlier this year, and he straightened me out fast. He said, 'I own this court when I'm out here. I'm the king bee.' I had to agree. I saw a picture in a magazine showing Reed knocking out Rudy LaRusso a few years ago, and I don't want to be knocked out in front of 19,500 people and a TV audience back home."

Milwaukee coach Larry Costello, a former NBA guard from the 1950s, had made a change before Game 3, starting veteran Fred Crawford in place of the aforementioned Flynn Robinson. Milwaukee won the game, but in the fourth game the Knicks took a commanding 20-point lead early. Then Robinson came in and helped the Bucks score 16 straight points to bring them all the way back to 69-67. It proved to be false hope for the young team. The Knicks turned on the afterburners and won going away, 117-105, with both Russell and Stallworth contributing big buckets off the bench.

The same night, April 19, on which the Knicks took a 3-1 lead over the Bucks, they learned which Western Division team would be in the finals. The Lakers and Wilt had completed a four-game sweep of the Atlanta Hawks. That gave the New Yorkers more impetus. They didn't want to let the Bucks hang around, get brazen, and make them work the way they did against the Bullets. The Lakers would be rested and ready, and the Knicks felt they had to wrap it up the following night at the Garden.

This one was the proverbial laugher. Barnett started hitting his jumper early, scoring nine points in the first three minutes and 16 by the end of the quarter. The game was over almost before it began. The Knicks had a 35-19 lead after one and just rolled from there, moving the ball with a slickness that hadn't been seen since early in the season, running all their plays to perfection and harassing the Bucks all over the floor. It was 69-45 at the end of the first half and 132-96 when the final buzzer sounded.

The fans were totally into the celebration. Before the game even ended they began chanting to Alcindor, *"Goodbye, Lewie, we hate to see you go! Goodbye, Lewie, we had to see you go!"* And organist Eddie Layton got into the act, playing "California Here We Come" as soon as the game ended.

FOUR MORE WINS

There isn't an athlete in any sport who doesn't want to play for a championship. That's the essence of team sports, to put your team in a position to win. The NBA is a long grind, a physically debilitating schedule that starts with the preseason, then continues through 82 regular-season games and, if you're lucky enough to get there, up to 21 additional contests in the postseasons. Thus a season can consist of more than 100 games of basketball, of running up and down the court, jumping, cutting, banging under the boards. It takes a toll. By the time a team is ready to play for the championship, no one feels 100 percent. Every single player has his share of aches and pains. Some have tender ankles, balky knees, sore ribs. Yet they go on.

Now the Knicks had reached that point, poised to take the final steps if they could just win four more games. Seems simple. Heck, they had won 18 straight at the beginning of the season. Four more must have seemed almost insignificant. But the final four games are often the toughest, because there's another team with the same feeling, the same hurts, the same long season, and the same desire to be called champions.

It would be the Knicks and the Lakers. The teams had met twice before, back in 1951-1952 and again the following year. The Lakers were in Minneapolis then, and those Knicks couldn't cope with the Lakers' super center, George Mikan. Now the Knicks would be meeting the Los Angeles Lakers. But as fate would have it, they would again have to cope with a super center, Wilt Chamberlain, whom many felt was the greatest player of all time.

Four more wins. In some respects, it must have felt a lifetime away.

CHAPTER 9

MEET THE LAKERS

MEET THE LAKERS

The Minneapolis Lakers were a dynasty; the Los Angeles Lakers were perennial bridesmaids, reaching the NBA Finals time and again only to be thwarted by Bill Russell and the Boston Celtics. The acquisition of Wilt Chamberlain prior to the 1968-1969 season was supposed to put the Lakers over the top, but they were once again beaten by Boston's last-hurrah team in the Finals. Now they were back. Chamberlain's return from his early-season knee injury was looked upon as miraculous. The Lakers hoped it was a sign that this was finally their year. The team finished two games behind the Atlanta Hawks in the Western Division with a 46-36 record, but with Wilt back they were certainly a different look to the ballclub.

The two perennial leaders of the Lakers were Jerry West and Elgin Baylor. But Baylor, one of the great forwards in NBA history, a guy who once averaged 38.3 points in a season, was 35 years old and had played just 54 games during the regular season.

But he was still good enough to toss in 24 a game and was ready for the playoffs. West, however, was a different story. The 6'3" guard out of West Virginia was nearly 32 years old but still playing at peak efficiency. He had led the NBA in scoring with a 31.2 average and was one of the great clutch shooters in the game. West could do it all. He was on the All-Defensive team as well as the All-NBA first team and was a player to be feared, especially in big games.

Playing the other forward was 6'7" Harold "Happy" Hairston, who came over in an early-season trade and was the team's leading rebounder in Chamberlain's absence. Hairston could also score, as his 18.5 season average attested. In his tenure with the Lakers he was a 20.6 scorer. But Hairston had a reputation for sometimes being a moody star, and word was that Happy wasn't as *happy* now that Wilt was back and occupying a large section of the floor where Hairston liked to operate. That was one of the questions coming in. Could Wilt and Hairston put it together on time?

The Lakers weren't especially deep. Young Dick Garrett was the other starting guard, and the team got some quality production from forward/guard Keith Erickson, 7'0" Mel Counts, who played more forward than center, and center Rick Roberson, who filled in during Chamberlain's absence. The team didn't have instant offense off the bench the way the Knicks did with Cazzie Russell, but the hope was that the starting five, especially the triumvirate of Chamberlain, West, and Baylor, could provide enough firepower to bring a championship to Los Angeles. The Lakers had lost to the Celtics six times in the Finals, a fact that could not escape the veteran players who had been through it. As Baylor said, "This doesn't seem real anyway. It seems to me that even if we get by the Knicks, the Celtics must be waiting for us somewhere out there."

More on the Guy from Cabin Creek

Jerry West deserves a special mention because he was a special player. Coming out of the tiny town of Cabin Creek, West Virginia, he went from being a rail-thin high school star to an All-American at the University of West Virginia. As a kid he would practice so hard and so long, that he would almost collapse. He would sometimes need special vitamin injections to keep healthy. He practiced in the cold weather with gloves, and when he finally joined the NBA Lakers he would always find himself in the shadow of the great Oscar Robertson. But West's greatness would eventually equal that of the Big O, and he would go on to have one of the great careers in NBA annals.

There were so many highlights. West, however, had always been a perfectionist, and no matter how well he played, he always felt he could play better. He once recalled a game in which he made 16 of 17 shots from the field and hit 12 straight free throws for a total of 44 points, had 12 rebounds, 12 steals, and 10 blocks. He had played a truly incredible game. Yet what did he say looking back at that night?

"Defensively, from a team standpoint, I didn't feel I played very well," he said. "Very rarely was I satisfied with how I played."

West was the man to fear in the playoffs. The bigger the game, the better he played, and there wasn't a guy in the league who would be chosen over West to take the last shot with the game on the line. In the 1965 Western Division Finals against Baltimore (then in the West), Baylor was injured in the first game, and without Elgin's presence, West scored 40 or more points in all six games, averaging an amazing 46.3 points, a record for a playoff series. For the entire postseason that year, he averaged 40.6 points, though the Lakers once again lost in the Finals to the Celtics.

In the 1969 Finals against Boston, the sharp-shooting guard averaged 37.9 points against the Celts and was named the Finals Most Valuable Player despite the fact that his team again lost. For these reasons, the Knicks knew that their ultimate nightmare might not be Wilt, but Jerry West. He never disappointed in the big game. In fact, West's philosophical approach to the game could be summed up when he retired. It was after the 1973-1974 season when a groin injury limited him to just 31 games and a 20.3 scoring average. When he announced he was leaving he said, among other things,

"I'm not willing to sacrifice my standards. Perhaps I expect too much."

THE STRATEGIES

It was no secret what the Knicks wanted to do. They had to play their aggressive defensive game and controlled offense. But with offensive giants like West, Baylor, and Chamberlain, defense would have to be paramount. All three were capable of putting up huge numbers, but in reality, Baylor was on the downside, and Wilt had been out most of the season. What they had done in the past wasn't an accurate gauge, but that didn't lessen the importance of the "D."

While the Knicks wanted to speed up the game to take advantage of the aging Baylor and the maybe still-gimpy Chamberlain, the Lakers wanted to slow it down. Laker coach Joe Mullaney added, "When [the Knicks] get us running, even I can't run with them, quick as I was." Though West was a great one-on-one player and Baylor had been one, the team preferred to slow the offense down, let Wilt get set underneath, and work off him. That was a change from what they had done earlier in the season, and the Knicks were hoping that the adjustment for the returning Chamberlain would disrupt the team chemistry.

Then there would be the battle of the centers. Reed was about four and a half inches shorter than Wilt but at least had the strength to duel with the 7'1", 290-pound behemoth. The captain's strategy was to try to keep Wilt from getting his high-percentage dunks. He planned to lean on the bigger man and try to force him a little farther from the hoop so that he would have to go with the fallaway jumper, which wasn't his best shot. Wilt definitely had more problems with bulky centers who liked to push and lean and not let him set up where he wanted. Bill Russell had been different. He often annoyed Wilt by keeping a hand on the big guy's lower back, but he also had the anticipation and quickness to beat Wilt to spots and block his shot more than any other center ever. But Reed wasn't Russell, and his strength was his biggest asset. Offensively, the range Willis had on his jumper could force Wilt outside to guard him and draw him away from the boards where no one could compete with him.

This was basically how it would begin. Maybe the key would be how each team would adjust. The Knicks had made changes against the Bullets and won the series. What no one knew before it began, nor could have possibly known, was just how radical an adjustment the Knicks would have to make.

GETTING STARTED

The Finals format was two games in New York followed by a pair in Los Angeles, and then if necessary, one, one, and one, which could mean three coast-to-coast flights in close proximity. That could be extremely tiring. But now everyone was concentrating on the April 24 opener at Madison Square Garden. After the noisy introductions from the gala New York crowd, it was time to play basketball. For the first two periods it looked like the early-season Knicks were back. They not only ran and moved the ball, but it was apparent that Reed was testing

Chamberlain's mobility. The captain was shooting from all around the key, daring Chamberlain to come out and get him. Better yet, he was hitting, and his 25 first-half points helped stake the Knicks to an 11-point lead.

Then in the third period the Lakers began coming back. West and Baylor were hitting their shots in a quietly efficient manner, and L.A. crept into contention. It was close for most of the final session as well, but the Knicks began to prevail in the closing minutes, led by one of those shooting streaks by Russell. Cazzie had eight points in a five-minute stretch, and the Knicks pulled away to win the opener handily, 124-112. Reed had 37 big points, while DeBusschere and the surprising Riordan had 19 apiece. Bradley and Barnett had 33 between them, showing off a balanced attack that seemed to grind the Lakers into submission.

CAN L.A. ADJUST?

The Lakers certainly had the horses to come back. You can never write off talents like West and Baylor, but the key was beginning to look as if it would be Chamberlain. Both Reed and Frazier didn't feel he was quite the same player. "I think he's still bothered by the knee," Willis said, after the game. "I don't know how much less mobile he is, but he can't move as fast on a drive. I don't think he reacts as quickly, and I don't think he can go up as high." When Frazier heard the captain's remarks and agreed, "He's lost a lot of movement," Clyde added. "I saw a couple of times when his knee gave out, and they called him for traveling because he was forced to take an extra step."

Coach Mullaney also felt his center had to move more. He couldn't sit underneath and allow Reed to roam free for those jump shots. Wilt was a player who had always done it his way. Some said he was more interested in his stats than in winning. Despite his acknowledged talent, which was awesome, he had been part of just a single championship team since coming into the league in 1959-1960. A big part of that was due to Bill Russell and the Celtics, so both Wilt and the Lakers were equal victims of the Celtics' success and now they were bound together to face the Knicks. Mullaney hoped his suggestions would get through to the big guy before the team met again three nights later.

GAME TWO

If nothing else, Wilt Chamberlain had pride. He didn't want to be torched for another 37 points, and for that reason he was infinitely more active in the second game. He blocked Reed's first shot of the night at the foul line and continued to dominate from there. His revival kept the game close. This one would go down to the final second as the teams appeared evenly matched throughout. Finally it came down to the Lakers having a 105-103 lead and the Knicks with the basketball looking for the tie.

Riordan had the ball, saw an opening, and began driving to the hoop with his usual abandon. Wilt quickly moved toward him, and seeing the big guy and his huge wingspan swooping in, Mike had second thoughts. He passed the ball back to Reed, who had to reach back for it. Then, with time running down, he went up for the shot. There was Chamberlain, high in the air, his long right arm blocking the shot in the lane. No foul. Buzzer. Game over. The Lakers had won it, 105-103. More importantly, they had won one at Madison Square Garden and shifted the home-court advantage to their side of the ball.

"That will give [Reed] something to think about," Wilt said, afterward. "Everyone thinks I'm crippled, but I guess I'm not. Do you think I worked four months on my knee so I could come here and jive? I came here to play!"

Now both teams boarded a plane for the flight to the left coast for Game 3 two nights later.

OUT IN MOVIELAND

Los Angeles has always been a strange sports town. The fans proclaimed their love for the Dodgers, yet Dodger Stadium was always half empty by the seventh inning as fans rushed to get a good place on the freeway. They loved the NFL Rams but gave them such spotty support that the team would eventually move to St. Louis. As for the Lakers, the Forum was the place where the stars like to show their faces, but the crowd didn't have the hard edge or knowledge of the game that New Yorkers had shown for so many years. Maybe it was because California was a Johnny-come-lately with professional sports, and everyone was still learning. Heck, the Dodgers had only been there for 12 years in 1970.

The consensus was that the fans then simply didn't have real passion for the game. You might see the likes of Walter Matthau, Dean Martin, Doris Day, Andy Williams, or Rhonda Fleming there, but you also found out that the team sold just 6,100 season tickets. If the fans in New York had that luxury every night, all those seats up for grabs on a game-to-game basis, the crowds outside Madison Square Garden would be huge. This was even before the days when Jack Nicholson became the number-one Lakers fan and could be seen at courtside every game.

That didn't mean the fans didn't want the home team to win. A championship would be yet another celebrity hook to hang a hat on, yet in larger-than-life Hollywood, Wilt got a bigger hand every night than Laker icons Baylor and West. For the Knicks, however, it didn't matter where the game was played. The court was still the same size, the baskets still ten feet high, and they had to win three more games to become champs.

THE SHOT OF A LIFETIME

The Knicks made one of those slight adjustments before Game 3, switching defensive assignments and putting Barnett on Jerry West. The feeling was that Barnett was the more physical defender than Frazier—hand checking, bumping, and pushing—while Clyde and his finesse resulted in more steals. With Frazier guarding Dick Garrett, who was not nearly the offensive threat West was, he'd be able to freelance and gamble more on getting a steal. The switch, Holzman felt, would also free Frazier up a bit more on offense. Frazier had to be encouraged to score sometimes. He himself said, "Shooting has never interested me that much." He was always the defender first, but had proven he could be a top scorer as well.

Barnett, who was a better defender than generally given credit for, did a nice job on West. His constant hand checking and jabbing had the Laker star so unnerved that he was called for several fouls when caught slapping Barnett's hand away. Dick, in turn, cooled on offense and missed all seven shots he took in the first half. Chamberlain was being active again on defense and led the Lakers to a 56-42 halftime lead. The Knicks seemed lethargic on offense and badly in need of a lift.

In the second half, the Knicks became more aggressive and began closing the gap. Barnett finally found his shooting touch in the final session, especially in the final four minutes. First he drove past West on the baseline, hit the hoop, and was fouled. His three-point play (the old-fashioned kind, a hoop and free throw) cut the Lakers' lead to 90-88. Then it became Barnett against the Lakers. When the score went to 96-96, the veteran guard had scored the last nine New York points. With the tension building, the two teams were tied at 100-all with the clock ticking down. The Knicks worked the ball, looking for the win. It ended up in DeBusschere's hands behind the foul line. A quick glance at the clock, and he went up with the jumper that dropped through the net with just three seconds left.

Chamberlain inbounded under the basket, flipping it to West. The veteran guard took the ball to the left side of the lane, dribbled three times, crouched, and launched a desperation 60-foot shot toward the basket at the other end of the floor. Almost the entire Knicks bench got up as if it was over, picking up towels and equipment to take off the court. Coach Holzman raised both his hands over his head.

THEN THE SHOT WENT IN!

The crowd at the forum erupted at what it had just seen. DeBusschere fell to the court under the L.A. basket. Legendary Lakers broadcaster Chick Hearn was screaming *"The Lakers tie it! The Lakers tie it! Oh my God!"* Everyone was in an uproar over West's amazing shot. Mr. Clutch had done it again. Only Knicks reserve Bill Hosket had a more clinical evaluation, one that made the shot even more incredible. Watching from the bench, Hosket said, "What's amazing was that West was concentrating on his follow through. I was watching him, and he shot the thing like he really figured it was going in."

OT

A last-second shot from 60 feet out can take the heart out of a team. It didn't win the game, but it certainly could have given the Lakers the feeling that, hey, we can't lose, and the Knicks a kick in the stomach from a bully who says you can't beat me. Both teams, however, had to face the reality that overtime is a fresh start, a five-minute period in which nothing that happened earlier counts. The score starts where it ended, but it just as easily could be 0-0 again.

Ironically, West's incredible 60-footer was his last basket of the night. Weary from going the entire distance and having

Barnett physically harass him, the great guard missed all five of his shots in overtime. Barnett was on the bench when the OT began, Riordan playing in his stead. Holzman finally brought him back with just 1:40 left. The Knicks led by one, 109-108, when Barnett took a pass from Reed some 10 feet from the hoop and promptly canned a jumper that turned out to be the final points of the game. The Knicks had won it, 111-108, taking back the home-court advantage they had given up in Game 2. Reed again put forth a great effort against Chamberlain, scoring 38 big points. He and Barnett were the heroes, yet when a reporter asked the veteran guard if his final shot, the one that sewed up the game, left him with a special feeling, Barnett turned and said casually, "No, not really."

THUMBS UP

There was more bad news for the Lakers after the game. West had apparently injured his left thumb in the first half when it banged up against Bradley's leg. Afterward, in the locker room, it had swelled up so much that he couldn't make a fist. The next morning the newspaper headlines read, WEST DOUBTFUL FOR GAME FOUR. None of the Knicks believed it. Along with all of his other talents, West was a gamer. As DeBusschere put it, "It's newspaper crap. No way he's not going to play."

Sure enough, when the teams lined up for the start of Game 4, West was standing out on the court ready to go. This one was an offensive explosion by both teams that again went into overtime. When it ended, the Lakers had tied the series at two games apiece, winning 121-115. And the hero was none other than Jerry West. Despite the so-called doubtful thumb, West scored 37 points and handed out 18 assists. Baylor turned back the clock and chipped in with 30. It turned out to be a thumbs up for the Lakers, especially from the guy with the bad thumb. But that was Jerry West, one of the truly great ones ever.

THE TUMBLE HEARD 'ROUND NEW YORK

This was still a series up for grabs. The two teams had battled through four games, two of them going to overtime, and were tied. Even though two of the final three games, if necessary, would be played at the Garden, it was far from an ironclad guarantee that the Knicks would win. In some ways, things weren't going well. The Lakers had begun using the quickness of Keith Erickson to harass Bill Bradley, and Dollar Bill had made just six of 24 shots in the two games on the coast. But even more worrisome to the Knicks was the condition of the captain.

Though Willis Reed had averaged 25.9 points and 15.9 rebounds in the playoffs thus far, his knees were becoming an increasing concern for the team's medical staff. It was now an open secret. Reed had tendinitis in both knees, and they weren't getting any better. Now the Knicks faced two games in three nights and perhaps three in five nights, with a possible pair of cross-country flights in between. On the court Willis had to play Wilt Chamberlain, who seemed to be getting stronger and was showing no signs of his surgically repaired knee giving out. The concern was not whether Willis would play, but whether he could continue playing effectively long enough against basketball's most powerful center for the Knicks to wrap up a title. But what was about to happen in the first quarter of Game 5 took everyone by surprise and shook the entire foundation that the Knicks had been building since the start of the season.

It was the Lakers who came out firing, playing with more energy than the Knicks, who looked inexplicably flat. In fact, L.A. had moved out to a 25-15 lead that had the large crowd at the Garden wondering when the real Knicks would decide to

stand up. Then with just 3:56 left in the opening quarter, Reed
got the basketball and made a move to drive past Chamberlain.
Wilt moved to cut him off, and somehow Willis tripped, going
down hard. It was said that even before he hit the floor he had
strained two muscles in his right thigh. In obvious pain, he was
helped off the court and then taken to the locker room by trainer
Whelan and Dr. James Parkes. The crowd at the Garden was
stunned to silence by the sight.

The thought of Reed not coming out for the second half was
almost incomprehensible. The captain was indestructible, wasn't
he? He's shake it off, most felt. But…what if he didn't?

An Amazing Adjustment

In the second quarter the Knicks struggled to stay in the
game. First Nate Bowman came in, but it was apparent he
couldn't do the job. Then Holzman tried Bill Hosket. Again, no
luck. Wilt was just overpowering them. Another timeout with
4:31 left in the half, and Holzman tried something else. When
the team returned to the floor, the 6'6" Dave DeBusschere was
matched up with Chamberlain. The team was still trying to see
what worked best while hoping Reed would come out to start the
second half. When the buzzer sounded at the end of the second
period, the Lakers had a 53-40 lead. The Knicks were still in it,
if just barely.

But once they reached the locker room they wondered if,
indeed, the series was over right there. They found their captain
still in severe pain, lying on a training table. It was not a
welcomed sight. The players were told immediately that Reed
would not be returning this night. Now Coach Holzman and his
charges had to talk strategy, and fast. Defensively, they would do
what they always did, but try to do it better. That meant being
quick, double-teaming when necessary and taking calculated

gambles to steal the ball, knock down passes, and disrupt the Lakers' offense as much as possible. Their offense was another story. Willis was an equalizer on offense, their only low post player, a guy who could erupt for 30 or more on any given night, and a broad body to set effective screens. Now he was gone.

Not surprisingly, it was Bill Bradley who got the brainstorm. Why not try a 1-3-1 offense? The 1-3-1 was an offense used mainly in college ball, often against zones. Here it would have to be used against a man to man. The way it would be set up Frazier would bring the ball up and be at the top of the offense (the 1). There would then be a pivot up high and two wingmen flanking him (the 3). The fifth man (the other 1), who would start down low, was called the "rover" or "roamer." This would be the man Wilt would have to guard. The rover would then come up high, forcing Wilt away from the hoop. In this case, the "rover" would be DeBusschere, and if Wilt didn't come out with him, in theory Dave would have an open shot. Barnett would be on one wing and the unselfish Bradley, always thinking team first, suggested that Russell be put on the other wing, because he was shooting better in the first half. Holzman thought a minute, then agreed. After some last-minute instructions, he told his team to go out and win it for the captain.

AN INCREDIBLE SECOND HALF

Hopes faded quickly when 19,500 fans didn't see the captain coming out for the start of the second half. But soon those same hopes were soaring again. The 1-3-1 offense seemed to be confusing the Lakers, and the defense continued to be the defense, even without the anchor that was Willis Reed. Joe Mullaney would later echo the confusion he saw on the court.

"They sped it up like a fast movie," the Lakers coach said. "We've been playing a certain style of game. All these playoff games have been nearly the same. Then, all of a sudden, it switches around a hundred percent."

Bill Bradley, the architect of the innovated strategy, put it this way. "Outside, we had two wings with a point man. Inside, we had one guy on the baseline and a roamer. When we saw Wilt not playing a man, it was like attacking a zone. Just hit the open spaces in a zone."

The defense was forcing the Lakers to places on the court where they didn't want to be, and they were having trouble getting good shots. Frazier, as was his habit, was on a defensive search-and-destroy mission, a one-man wrecking crew for minutes at a time. This phase of the game still turned Clyde on more than scoring points. Chamberlain, with DeBusschere still on him, seemed to have disappeared into the same murky place his teammates had gone. The Knicks began closing the gap. At the end of three the Los Angeles lead was down to 82-75.

At the start of the fourth quarter DeBusschere somehow continued to contain Chamberlain. He leaned on him and tried to keep the big guy from moving toward the basket. Then, with 9:17 left, Double D picked up his fifth foul. Holzman took yet another chance. He sent the 6'7" Dave Stallworth in to guard Wilt. Stallworth didn't have the bulk to lean on Wilt. He wouldn't even try. Instead he altered the tempo. DeBusschere had been physical with Wilt, just as Reed had. Stallworth was elusive, moving quickly from side to side behind Wilt, as if he were trying to hide behind a big tree and not be seen. Because Wilt couldn't keep track of him, didn't always know where he was, it seemed to confuse him.

A Bradley jumper tied the game at 87-87 with 7:43 left. The Knicks had caught the Lakers, and they were doing it without Willis Reed. Then with 5:19 remaining, Bradley drained yet another jumper, giving the Knicks the lead for the first time, 93-91. The Lakers weren't responding—not Wilt, not Baylor, not even Jerry West. They simply had not adjusted to the unorthodox moves of the Knicks. Russell came in to hit six straight, and Stallworth continued to play one of his best games of the year, especially on defense, which was not his strong point. From there the Knicks coasted home with an improbable 107-100 victory, giving them a 3-2 lead in the series. It was a victory not even the most reckless of bettors would have wagered on after Reed went down and didn't return. But this had been a resourceful, opportunistic team all year, and they had defied the odds once again.

Amazingly, Wilt Chamberlain had only four second-half points, and Jerry West took just two shots in the second half. So disgusted was West that he was heard to say afterward, "I've seen two good drinkers take more shots than [we did] in one evening."

For Dave DeBusschere, this game would always have a lasting impact. Some 20 years later, the great power forward would say, "The fifth game was one of the greatest basketball games ever played." Boston Celtics great John Havlicek agreed, calling it "the greatest comeback in basketball."

Now the shuttle was on its way back to L.A. The Lakers certainly had to question their character and resolve, as well as their ability to adjust. But the Knicks had more worries than that. They still didn't know whether Willis Reed would suit up again in the playoffs. And if he couldn't, how long could they bluff and fool the Lakers without their big man? They still hoped they wouldn't have to find out.

BLOWOUT

The captain made the trip to Los Angeles, but that's all he did. There was no way he could play. In fact, he even had trouble walking. The official diagnosis was a strain of the tensor and the rectus femoris, two muscles, the latter being the one that runs from the pelvis across the hip to the knee. Reed was being given all kinds of treatment but had yet to respond. The ideal treatment, of course was complete rest. That begged another *what if.* What if the Knicks lost Game 6 and then faced the single biggest game in franchise history, a seventh and deciding game for the championship? Could Reed manage to play in that one and, if so, how effective would he be?

But first things first. Everyone expected the Knicks, minus their captain, would come out with the same kind of alignment that had worked to perfection in Game 5. Why not try to win it by driving the Lakers to distraction with speed, defense, and that 1-3-1 offense? Up to now, the Lakers had proved to be a team that couldn't adjust. They played basically one way. When they had it all working and the big guy was doing his thing, they won. As soon as there was a fly in the ointment, they seemed to come apart. The Knicks players knew this, and that's why most of them were surprised, almost shocked, to hear their coach say that Nate Bowman would be starting at center. It was almost as if Holzman decided to concede Game 6 and hope Reed would be back for the last one.

When the team took the floor, Bill Bradley stayed behind to try to convince Holzman to stay with the lineup and strategy that had worked so well in Game 5, but the veteran coach wouldn't listen this time. He just didn't want to hear it. The Lakers must have been salivating with anticipation when they saw the Knicks come out with a conventional lineup. With their confidence restored immediately, the Lakers romped. Wilt was shooting from the start, Dick Garrett made his first eight shots, and everyone contributed. The Lakers won easily 135-113, with Wilt scoring 45 to go with 27 rebounds, and West adding 33 and 13 assists. As for the Knicks, they offered only token resistance, obviously dispirited as much by their coach's strategy as by the Lakers shot-making. The series was tied once more, and everyone would have to take a final flight back to New York.

WOULD HE OR WOULDN'T HE?

With just a day between games, the speculation, the questions, the guesses, and the predictions were non-stop. The switchboard at the Garden rang continuously. People not only wanted to know if Reed was going to play, but some were calling with all kinds of homemade and strange "cures." Medically, Willis was having conventional treatment for strained muscles—ultrasounds, massage, hot packs, and whirlpools.

You would think that the Lakers could have flown to New York without a plane. They had won Game 6 going away, and knew, in their hearts, that even if Reed played, there was no way he could be close to 100 percent. Maybe it was an unfair advantage, but that was the crapshoot that often characterized sports. Injuries were an X-factor and had sabotaged many teams over the years. It could happen to you, or it could happen to your opponent. No matter which side of the fence you were on, you didn't stop playing. The championship was still at stake. Yet you had to wonder what his Laker teammates felt when the Los Angeles *Herald-Examiner* ran a headline on its sports page quoting Wilt Chamberlain. It read:

WE AMERICANS EMPHASIZE WINNING TOO MUCH

Hey, what was that all about? The team was on the brink of an elusive title, and the star center, who worked his butt off to get back for the playoffs was suddenly saying it doesn't really matter if you win. On the other side of the fence there was Willis Reed, struggling to be ready, doing all he could so that he could be ready and try to help his team win. Wilt seemed to be going back to the give-it-the-old-college-try adage that said, *"It's not whether you win or lose, but how you play the game."* That had to leave a guy like Jerry West, who put it all out there every night, wondering what was next.

On game day there was still no announcement about the captain's status. In New York City, people forgot about the daily financial fluctuations at the Stock Exchange, they didn't care which shows were opening or closing on Broadway, they weren't worried about which restaurant they might visit that night, or how crowded their favorite watering hole might be at game time. Only one question was on the mind of anyone remotely interested in sports.

Would Willis Reed play?

Reed's teammates knew their captain would be on the court if there was any possible way for him to do it. They had heard him say, "I'll play if I have to crawl." The question was how effective could he be? What if he played and he hurt them? They couldn't imagine the captain trying to give it a go and Holzman being forced to pull him out of the game. Reed recalled the emotion he felt years later.

"I wanted to play," he said. "That was for the championship, the one great moment you play for all your life. I didn't want to have to look at myself in the mirror 20 years later and say I wished I had tried to play."

But then there were the obvious restrictions and the pain. The Garden was still empty except for employees when Reed walked slowly onto the court just after 6 p.m. Don May came with him and began feeding him the ball. The captain began arching a few shots up from different spots on the floor. He was favoring his leg and not really jumping. But at least he was out there. From an entranceway to the locker room a tall, goateed man was watching in silence. No one will ever know just what Wilt Chamberlain was thinking at that very minute.

Still, there had been no official announcement as to Reed's status and game time was just a couple of hours away.

EMOTION RIDES HIGH

When the Knicks finally took the floor, Reed wasn't there. The capacity crowd watched carefully as the players filed out ready to erupt with the appearance of the captain. But no dice. The Lakers were looking as well. Still, there was no official announcement. Though none of the fans at the Garden that night knew it, Reed was still in the locker room with Dr. Parkes, and the two were making sure just where the pain was. Then the doctor would carefully give him another cortisone shot, which was an anti-inflammatory, as well as an injection of Carbocaine to kill the pain. Only Cazzie Russell had stayed behind to be with him

The fans continued to watch the entrance to the court, and when they saw someone coming through they began to cheer. Then they realized it was Cazzie. Still no captain. But within minutes another figure came out of the tunnel. Again everyone looked. This time there was no mistake about it. Willis Reed was walking gingerly onto the court. Madison Square Garden erupted. It's doubtful that the old arena, throughout its three incarnations, was ever louder. Even the Lakers stopped their warmup drills and just watched. The drama was unmistakable, and no matter what followed, there was a good chance it would affect the outcome of the game. Some of the Knicks noticed it immediately.

"I saw the whole Laker team standing around staring at this man," Walt Frazier said. "When I saw that, when they stopped warming up, something told me we might have these guys."

As for the rest of the Knicks, they all breathed a sigh of relief, as well. The captain was out there with them for the biggest game of their lives. They didn't know how much he would contribute, but two things were certain. His presence would give them a huge lift, and had probably already somewhat deflated the

Lakers. Secondly, no matter how badly he felt, Reed would give everything he had. By that time the entire league knew about the captain's determination. Tough Bill Bridges of the Atlanta Hawks probably expressed it best when he said, "There is not one other guy in the league that gives the 100 percent that Reed does every night, every game of the season, at both ends of the court."

TIME TO PLAY

When the starting teams came out onto the court, Reed was with them. He wasn't just there to make a token appearance, a way to boost the morale of his team. He was there to start the game. Reed shook hands with Chamberlain, who had come into the series as the wounded warrior but now would likely have a huge advantage. Yet in the first two minutes of the game it was Reed who made the definitive statement. He came down court slowly the first time the Knicks had the ball, took a pass, and promptly hit a jump shot from behind the key. The Garden erupted again. Minutes later he again trailed the play, took a pass, and hit a 20-footer from the right wing.

Defensively, he began leaning on Wilt, using his bulk and strength to keep the bigger man away from the basket. Chamberlain, at this stage of his career, was not especially mobile and never took advantage of the fact that Reed had almost no lateral movement. The Knicks extended the lead to 9-2 before Baylor hit a basket. Then a basket by Bradley, a pair of foul shots from Frazier, and a jumper from DeBusschere ran it to 15-6. After Chamberlain slammed home an offensive rebound, Bradley went in for a lay-up and the Knicks led, 17-8.

It was apparent already that the Lakers had not adjusted to Reed's limited presence. Everyone could see that Reed was moving with great difficulty, dragging his right leg. But Joe Mullaney never changed the offense, never went to movement as

Walt Frazier had one of the great games in NBA annals when the Knicks clinched the title against the Lakers. He scored 36 points and had 19 assists in the most important game of the season. Photo by Vernon J. Biever

the Knicks had done when Willis first went down. Chamberlain kept playing his stationary game that allowed Reed to be effective enough to allow the Knicks to take the early lead and renew their confidence.

Then, slowly, with great support from the other starters, Walt Frazier began taking over the game. Not only was his playing his usual strong, lurking defense, and looking for the open man on offense, he was also creating shots, hitting five in the row in the first quarter alone. The defense was making steals, even swiping the ball from the usually impeccable West as Frazier made a move from behind Mike Riordan (who was guarding West) and pilfered the ball at midcourt. The Lakers had 15 turnovers in the first half alone, and when the buzzer sounded at the end of the second period the Knicks had a 69-42 lead, totally in the driver's seat and just 24 minutes from their first championship.

CLOSING THE DEAL

Reed took yet another painkilling shot at halftime, but he wouldn't be needed much longer. Frazier continued to control the game, and the Lakers failed to adjust once again. When they showed signs of making a run early in the third quarter Frazier personally turned it around. He hit a jump shot, a free throw, stole the ball and scored, stole it again and scored, and when his spurt ended, the Knicks' lead was back up to 79-54. By then it was safe to remove the captain from the game. He came to the bench to another thunderous standing ovation, having played 27 courageous minutes. He had scored only four points, those first two baskets, but he had effectively defended the immobile Chamberlain with his bulk and guile, and his teammates did the rest.

They continued the pressure right through the final session, finally coasting in the last minutes, savoring the moments, the cheers of the crowd, and the feeling that goes with knowing you are minutes away from a championship. It ended at 113-99, the final score not really indicative of the total domination the Knicks had exhibited for 48 minutes. Then the buzzer sounded, and the celebration began.

Reed was announced as the Finals MVP, completing a year in which he was also the regular season's Most Valuable Player and the MVP of the mid-season All-Star Game. In a sense, his dramatic appearance and gutsy performance masked the final game played by Walt Frazier. Clyde had fully justified his selection to the NBA First Team and the All-NBA Defensive team. All he did against the Lakers that night was score 36 points on 12 of 17 from the field and a perfect 12 of 12 from the foul line. He also added a playoff record-tying 19 assists (Bob Cousy and Wilt had also done it), numerous steals, and defensive gems. It was one of the great seventh-game performances in NBA history.

DeBusschere was also great. In his quietly efficient way he finished with 18 points and 17 rebounds, while Barnett scored 21 and held West to nine-of-19 shooting. Bradley popped for 16, giving the quartet 91 of the Knicks 113 points. Once again, as had been the case all year, it was a total team effort. Afterward, almost all the talk was about the all-out, pain-filled effort of the captain.

"The courage Willis demonstrated was his faith in us," Bill Bradley said. "His courage is incredible. I had chills before the game. Willis not only played on one leg, he kept Wilt from hitting. All we wanted from him was defense. And then he hit his first two shots and I said, 'Hold on a minute. Maybe he's got something else.'"

Dick Barnett put it this way: "I feel real proud. But Willis was something else. Everyone was on pins and needles waiting on him. Even L.A. was watching the corridor for him to come out. It has to have some effect on them."

"He could barely walk, and we asked him to run," said Cazzie Russell.

Dave DeBusschere felt great for the entire team. "It's hard to explain, there's so much emotion," he said, afterward. "Willis getting hurt was a major setback, but this proved we could come back. It proved what a great team we are."

Reed himself, who hated to give in to pain as much as to an opposing center, admitted his 27-minute stint took a real effort. "It was rough," he said. "The legs started to hurt from the opening jump."

As for the usually laconic coach, even Red Holzman was moved by the captain's sacrifice. "He gave us a tremendous lift just going out there," Holzman said. "He couldn't play his normal game, but he did a lot of things out there. And he means a lot to the spirit of the other players. Willis rates with the greatest in courage. But that's what you can expect for him."

As for the Lakers, they had been frustrated in the Finals once again, only this time by another team. Their general manager, Fred Schaus, pointed out what many already knew. "We lost the series in the fifth game," he said. "We had our big chance and blew it." Wilt Chamberlain, whose surprising return from knee surgery gave Los Angeles a real chance to win admitted the Knicks were the better team. But he said something that many Knicks fans were already thinking about.

"They were just great," Wilt said. "Let's say they are the greatest now, because they won and we lost. But they'll have to win a couple more titles before they can be compared with the Boston Celtics."

That may have been true. But did it matter at that moment? Heck, no. All that mattered was that the Knicks had done it. They had won an NBA championship for the first time, had done it with style and grace, overcoming adversity, and showing everyone in the sport what a team that's totally together can accomplish. It was surely a moment to be savored and of which to be proud. And it was one that would not only live forever in the city of New York, but in the whole history of the NBA, as well. It was truly a signature victory.

CHAPTER 10

A GREAT TITLE AND BEYOND

HEROES

It was a championship for the ages. The team had fulfilled the bright promise of a 23-1 start, rallying from adversity several times during the season and finally from the greatest possible adversity—losing its captain and leader in the midst of the championship series only to have him re-emerge in the final game to inspire the team to its ultimate victory. What a team; what a season; what a championship! The Knicks were the toast of New York.

Reed, Frazier, Bradley, DeBusschere, Barnett, Russell, Stallworth, Riordan, et al. They could have written their own tickets. They owned the Garden, and they owned the town. Not only was it the Knicks' first title ever. The team had inherited the mantle of the Boston Celtics, a team that had won 11 titles in 13 years. That would never happen again, but those watching the way the Knicks performed easily saw them repeating the following season and maybe winning a few more after that. As

It was a long time coming. Captain Willis Reed and coach Red Holzman hold the NBA championship trophy after the Knicks won their first title ever in seven games over the Lakers. AP/WWP

Walt Frazier said at a special victory party for the team the night after their greatest victory, "We'll do it again next year."

Others agreed. Losing coach Joe Mullaney, whose failure to adjust after Reed's injury lessened his team's chances of winning, felt the Knicks weren't through yet. "This could be the start of a dynasty in New York," Mullaney said. "The Knicks are a young team and fit together like a jig-saw puzzle. They fit together perfectly. I'm sure Eddie Donovan and Red Holzman fitted them together piece by piece. It's the only way a team like this could have happened."

Was this a special team? Yes, they were, because they brought such a total team concept to the NBA, winning differently than the Celtics, for example, a team that relied on a super center (Bill Russell) who was a defensive force all by himself, and a fast-breaking offense. The Knicks did it together, each player having the ability to rise to the occasion when necessary. And they could adjust, change their style to fit an opponent or to compensate for their own shortcomings. But would they do it again? Only time would tell. Too many things can happen in professional sports to make predictions of the future.

DYNASTIES HARD TO COME BY

The Knicks victory gave New York its third championship in 17 months, following on the heels of the Jets' triumph over the Colts in January of 1969 and the Mets' win over the Orioles the following October. Oddly enough, the only professional team in the city to have a dynasty was the baseball Yankees, and they had been in a rare down period since 1965. So the door was open. Unfortunately, neither the Jets nor Mets were able to follow through on their greatest seasons. Joe Namath's Jets lost to Kansas City, 13-6, in the playoffs following the 1969 season. They would never reach the Super Bowl again.

The Mets, after that surprisingly magical season, had three mediocre, third-place finishes, lost their manager, Gil Hodges, to a heart attack, then made it back to the World Series in 1973, though finishing the regular season only three games over .500 (82-79), before losing the Series to the A's. They wouldn't win again until 1986 when there was a totally different team in place. There's an old adage in sports that applies to both individuals as well as entire teams. It says, in effect, that getting there is tough enough, staying there is even tougher.

The Knicks would learn that lesson very quickly.

WHAT HAPPENED NEXT

The Knicks would remain a top-echelon team for another four years, and in spite of winning a second NBA title in 1972-73, they would never again regain the magic of 1969-1970. A big part of that would be the deteriorating health of Willis Reed. In 1970-1971, the league expanded from 14 to 17 teams and realigned itself into four divisions. The Knicks were in the East with Boston, Philadelphia, and the new Buffalo team. Old rival Baltimore was in the Central, Milwaukee was in the Midwest and, of course, the Lakers remained out West.

When the season ended, the Knicks had won the East with a 52-30 record, a falloff of eight games from the season before. Milwaukee at 66-16 was the only team with a better record. Many felt the team would again rise in the playoffs. They were still tops defensively, but the Bucks had, by far, the greatest average margin of victory, 12.2 points a game. Still, many felt the veteran Knicks, with essentially the same club, would again dominate the playoffs. The team beat Atlanta handily in the semifinals, and then went up against old rival Baltimore. After winning the first two, then leading 3-2 after five, it wound up in a seventh game at the Garden, and the Bullets pulled it out, 93-

91, shocking both the Knicks and their fans. There would be no repeat title. The Bucks, led by Kareem Abdul-Jabbar (Lew Alcindor) would win the title by sweeping the Bullets in four straight games.

A year later the team began to change. Cazzie Russell and Mike Riordan were gone, and in a shocking trade, Earl "The Pearl" Monroe joined the Knicks. Some thought he'd never mesh with Frazier or be a Holzman kind of player, but the Pearl showed he could play defense and joined Clyde to form a great backcourt. Only he wasn't the freewheeling, freelancing scorer he had been. Veteran center/forward Jerry Lucas also came over. On the downside, Reed played just 11 games due to tendinitis in his left knee. Without the captain, the team finished second to the revived Celtics in the East at 48-34, then lost to the Bullets in six games in the playoff semi-finals as Wilt and the Lakers finally won that elusive title. The Lakers also ran off an incredible, 33-game win streak, obliterating the Knicks' record, and finishing the regular season with a record 69-13 mark. For the New Yorkers, it looked as if the team was going downhill.

A SECOND TITLE

Reed was back in 1972-1973 but was obviously not the player he used to be. He played in 69 games, averaged just 11 points and grabbed only 590 rebounds. Frazier, DeBusschere, Bradley, and Monroe were the stars, and the club finished 57-25, 11 games behind the Celtics' league-best 68-14. But in the playoffs, the New Yorkers turned back the clock. They beat the Bullets in five games, then upset the Celtics in seven. They got a break when Celtics star John Havlicek was hurt and couldn't play in the deciding game. Finally they beat the Lakers again, this time in five, and Reed played well enough to be named the Finals MVP. The team wouldn't be a dynasty, but the same core group had brought a second title to New York, and even though it didn't have the same kind of charismatic drama of the first championship, it was still special. But it was also a last hurrah.

The team was 49-33 in 1973-1974, but Reed played just 19 games. His knees were shot. The rest of the core group tried, but they were getting older. They beat the renamed Capital Bullets in seven games, but then were taken out by the eventual champs, the Celtics, in five. A year later, with Reed retired and the team, now changing, finished at 40-42. In a new playoff format they were beaten by Houston in a preliminary best-of-three format. The run was finally over.

TRACKING THE PLAYERS

The 1969-1970 Knicks are still looked upon as one of the great teams in NBA history. Great teams, of course, also need great players, and the Knicks certainly had their share. The starters on the 1969-1970 team, as well as sixth man Cazzie Russell, all had outstanding careers and continued to achieve when their playing days were done. The lessons learned while competing at sports on both the collegiate and professional levels often carry over to post-athletic life if the individual takes in everything he sees, hears, and learns. While winning is certainly the prime focus, even at the collegiate level, there are other lessons to be taken from sports, as well.

Players don't have to be close friends with all their teammates, but they must work together on the field or on the court. Teams have a mixed bag of personalities, players from different areas of the country, from different backgrounds, different races and religions. The successful player can come away from his sport with more than statistics, honors, championships, and memories. He can retire with the knowledge to continue to achieve, contribute, and give back during the remainder of his working days. Players in the 1960s and 1970s didn't make the millions of dollars paid to today's players. Most had to continue working when their playing careers were done. That was the case with the 1969-1970 Knicks.

Let's see the roads they traveled once their playing careers ended.

THE CAPTAIN

Sabotaged by bad knees, Willis Reed never had another truly great season after the 1969-1970 championship. Though he was definitely in decline in 1972-1973, he contributed to the Knicks' second title season and was Finals MVP once more. He played just 19 games the following year and then announced his retirement. In 10 seasons he averaged 18.7 points a game and grabbed more than 8,000 rebounds. Had his knees held up, his career would have undoubtedly lasted longer and his numbers would have been better. But that really doesn't matter.

Willis will be forever remembered for limping onto the court for Game 7 against the Lakers and inspiring his teammates to victory. In 1976 he became the first Knicks player to have his number retired, and in 1982 was enshrined in the Basketball Hall of Fame. Since his retirement, Willis has stayed very much connected to the game he loves. He has served as both an assistant coach at St. John's University and the head coach at Creighton University. In 1985 he was back in the NBA as an assistant coach with the Atlanta Hawks and then the Sacramento Kings. In February of 1988 he became the head coach of the New Jersey Nets, and by 1993 was the Nets general manager, and finally, in 1996, he became the senior vice president of basketball operations.

After 15 years with the Nets, Willis joined the Knicks front office prior to the 2003-04 season. Unfortunately, he didn't stay

with his old team for long. A year later he went home to
Louisiana to become the vice president of basketball operations
for the New Orleans Hornets. So Willis Reed has spent a life in
basketball and today is one of the most respected figures in the
game. Yet whenever people think of him, they still think first of
that night in 1970 when everyone waited to see if he'd come out
onto the court. All these years later he still says, "There isn't a day
in my life that people don't remind me of that game."

CLYDE

Walt Frazier would make the All-Defensive first team for six
years in a row, starting with the championship year of 1969-
1970. For a guy from Southern Illinois who was considered
something of a risk when he was drafted, he went on to become
an all-time great player. Even when the Knicks began declining
after the 1972-1973 season, Frazier continued his all-star brand
of play. In 1975, he was the MVP of the All-Star game with a 30-
point performance. But by 1976-1977 his scoring average was
down to 17.4, and the Knicks missed the playoffs for the second
straight season.

Then, on the eve of the 1977-1978 season, he was
ignominiously sent to the Cleveland Cavaliers as compensation
for the Knicks' signing of free-agent Jim Cleamons. When he left
the Knicks, Clyde was the Knicks' all-time leader in scoring,
assists, games played, and minutes. Patrick Ewing would
ultimately surpass him in all those categories except assists. In
Cleveland, Clyde was hampered by foot injuries and played just
66 more games over three seasons before he was waived three
games into the 1979-1980 campaign.

For his career, Walt Frazier averaged 18.9 points a game and
had more than 5,000 assists. But all those steals, all those clutch
defensive maneuvers are remembered today as much or more

than his scoring. And that's fine with Clyde. After retirement, Frazier spent some time as a player agent, was an investor in the United States Basketball League, which didn't last long, and later moved to the U.S. Virgin Islands where, of all things, he earned a charter boat captain's license.

When he lost his home and boat to Hurricane Hugo, he moved back to New York, and in 1989 began working as an analyst on Knicks broadcasts and telecasts. Not unexpectedly, he forged his own style and still delights listeners with his colorful rhymes and descriptions of today's players and games. In 1987, Walt Frazier was elected to the Basketball Hall of Fame, and in 1996 was named to the NBA 50th Anniversary All-Time team. Even today, Clyde prefers to talk about defense when someone asks him about the way he played the game.

"I didn't believe in contact defense," he explained. "I liked to keep them guessing where I was. I had the advantage because my hands were so quick. It was like playing possum. I was there, but I didn't look like I was there. [My opponents] relaxed more than if I was up there pressuring them all the time. That was when they got careless."

BRADLEY

What happened with Bill Bradley is no secret. Teammates used to kid him that he would be president some day. He didn't quite get there, but with his Princeton and Oxford background, he was obviously destined for more. He wound up a three-term United States senator from New Jersey on the democratic side of the aisle beginning in 1980. After leaving the Senate he made an aborted run for the democratic presidential nomination in 1999, but could not build up a real groundswell of support and, after losing to eventual candidate Al Gore in several key primaries, he dropped out and returned to private life.

But the man called Dollar Bill certainly had an interesting run with the Knicks. As a ballplayer, Bradley also had an interesting career. As with anything else he ever did, Bill Bradley worked at his game and became the best player he could possibly be. He never achieved the same superstar status he had at Princeton, but he was an integral and important part of the two Knicks title teams and a fine player in his own right. Jeff Mullins, an All-Star guard with the San Francisco Warriors summed up Bradley's work ethic back in 1970 when he said, "I've never seen a guy work as hard as he does to get open."

Bradley was always the thinking man's player. He was the architect of the successful 1-3-1 offense in Game 5 when Reed went down. In other words, this was a guy you would want on your ballclub. After getting his late start due to his tenure at Oxford, Bradley played 10 seasons with the Knicks. He kept his incredible consistency through 1975-1976. Then, in his final season of 1976-1977, he began tapering off to a part-timer who averaged just 4.3 points a game. He knew it was time to go and also knew he had bigger fish to fry.

He left the Knicks with a 12.4 career scoring average, which at first glance doesn't appear so impressive. But Bill Bradley meant a lot more to the team than just points, and those who knew the game recognized that quality. In 1983 he was rewarded with induction to Basketball's Hall of Fame. The risk the Knicks took drafting Bradley and the wait for him to finish his tenure at Oxford certainly paid huge dividends.

DeBusschere

The working man's forward was simply one tough character. For 12 years Dave DeBusschere battled the best and strongest forwards of his time, and there were plenty of good ones back them. His work ethic was second to none, and he came to play every night. With DeBusschere on the court you never had to worry about the kind of game you would get. Toughness, determination, consistency. They were all benchmarks of his game. In the Knicks' second championship season of 1972-1973, he still averaged 16.3 points a game and grabbed more than 10 rebounds a night. A year later, with the Knicks still good enough to win 49 games he averaged 18.1 points, second best of his career, and then retired. Not coincidentally, the following year the team plummeted to 40-42. You just don't replace a Dave DeBusschere in the blink of an eye.

In 12 seasons, DeBusschere scored 14,053 points for an average of 16.1 a game. He also averaged more than 10 rebounds a game for his career. But he did much more than that. As Red Holzman once said of his tough forward, "I didn't realize he was as good as he was until we got him. I always knew he was an outstanding player, but not this good. [But sometimes] you don't realize how good a guy is until you see him play every night." Fittingly, Dave DeBusschere was inducted into the Hall of Fame in 1983, the same year as his fellow forward, Bill Bradley. It was an honor fully deserved.

Though he had offers, DeBusschere did not want to return to coaching. "My coaching experience at such a young age was one of the best things that happened to me," he said, "but I wouldn't want to go back to coaching."

But he did stay in the game. In 1974 he served as vice president and general manager of the ABA New York Nets. A year later he was named commissioner of the American Basketball League and helped the young league secure a merger with the NBA. DeBusschere returned to the Knicks in 1982 as a VP and director of basketball operations. He was on the podium when the first ever NBA draft lottery was held in 1986. The Knicks won it and had the first choice that Dave quickly used to select Georgetown center Patrick Ewing. He left the job shortly afterward. In 1996 he was named to the NBA's 50th Anniversary

All-Time team. Years later, DeBusschere was reminiscing with a reporter when he summed up his tenure with the Knicks.

"Sometimes you hear old guys in sports say they didn't know how good they had it," he said. "I knew how good I had it. We all did."

DeBusschere remained in the New York area, and then on May 14, 2003, the city and the entire Knickerbocker family received a tragic shock. Dave DeBusschere had collapsed on a Manhattan street and died shortly afterward at NYU Downtown Hospital. He had suffered a massive heart attack. Except for Coach Holzman, who died in 1998, DeBusschere was the first member of the title teams to pass away. Bill Bradley had once said that as a player, DeBusschere was irreplaceable. As a man, it was the same. Perhaps it was his old foe, Earl Monroe, later a teammate, who caught the essence of DeBusschere's passing when he said, "Basketball is what united us. Friendship is what kept us together all these years. Only we understand what a great teammate he was. Red [Holzman] was the dad. We were the kids. And then we loved growing old together."

BARNETT

Dick Barnett was probably the unsung hero of the Knicks' first title run. A true professional, he did his job without fanfare, without attracting the attention usually reserved for Reed, Frazier, Bradley, and DeBusschere. But Barnett was a fine, all-around player, an underrated defender as well as a fine scorer. His career began in 1959 when he joined the old Syracuse Nats. He went on to play 14 NBA seasons, not including one year in the ABA (1961-1962) when he led the Cleveland Pipers to an ABA title. He then played for the Lakers and finally the Knicks, retiring after playing just five games in the 1973-1974 season. For his career he averaged 15.8 points a game with a high of 23.1

in 1965-1966. But on any given night he was capable of erupting for 30 or more with his unorthodox left-handed jumper.

Barnett has never made the Basketball Hall of Fame, but in February of 2005 he was inducted into the Tennessee Sports Hall of Fame for his fine play at Tennessee State University. TSU Athletic Director Teresa Phillips said, "We are honored to celebrate the premier basketball player in TSU's proud athletic history. Dick Barnett was a leader on and off the court. I think it is fitting that the first jersey retired by the TSU basketball program is Dick Barnett's number 35. It is a tribute fitting of his legendary status."

Barnett remains TSU's all-time leading scorer with 3,009 career points, but he's not a guy to look back. He was an assistant coach for the Knicks for a short time, then left the NBA. Surprisingly cerebral, something the general public didn't know during his playing days, Barnett earned his degree at Tennessee State, went on to earn a second degree from New York University, and finally received his doctorate from Fordham University. His postcareer work has always been designed to help others.

He has done a lot of work for the Athletic Role Model Educational Institution, an organization that seeks to enhance self-esteem among young African Americans. In addition, he has served as a professor of sports management at St. John's University. In 1990, the New York Knicks finally honored the contributions of Dick Barnett by retiring his jersey.

CAZZIE

Cazzie Russell was a sometimes starter, sometimes sixth man, but always electric. A great streak shooter, he could always create excitement, and Garden fans cheered in anticipation whenever he entered the game. Unfortunately, Cazzie was gone when the team won a second title in 1972-1973. He had been traded to Golden

State in 1971-1972 and promptly averaged 21.4 points for the Warriors and became an All-Star. Two years later he scored at a 20.5 clip. Maybe he never quite recaptured the glory of his college days, but in a 12-year career that also included a stint with the Lakers and a final season with the Bulls, Caz averaged 15.1 point a game.

Upon his retirement Cazzie became a sports analyst for CBS TV's *NBA Game of the Week*. He later began coaching in some of the developmental leagues and finally found his niche by becoming the head basketball coach at the Savannah College of Art and Design where he has coached for nearly a decade. Under his leadership the program has improved to the point where the school has gone from an NAIA program to a full NCAA Division III program in 2003. His 2002-2003 had a 21-6 record and school-record 16 wins in a row. Cazzie should know something about win streaks. After all, he played a big part in the Knicks' 18-game win streak to start their magical championship run in 1969.

THE COACH

William "Red" Holzman was old school, a coach who grew up with the NBA, played during the league's infancy and began coaching as the league moved into the realm of big-time sports. He would continue to coach the Knicks through the 1981-1982 season when he was nearly 62 years old. Red's final coaching record with the Knicks was 613-384, making him the winningest coach in franchise history. Not only was he named Coach of the Year in 1970, but he was also was named NBA Coach of the Decade for the 1970s. His Knicks teams won a pair of championships, and his defensive-oriented team style of play was very successful at the time when the league was full of great players, superstars who loved to go one on one. Red would have none of that and got the message across to his team. That message was simple: "If you play good, hard defense, the offense will take care of itself."

In 1986, Holzman's achievements were recognized when he was inducted into the Basketball Hall of Fame, where he now joins four of his top players from his great title teams of 1970 and 1973. Holzman was the author of four books after his retirement and died on November 13, 1998, at the age of 78.

IN RETROSPECT

Why were the 1969-1970 Knicks so special? For one thing, they were the right team for the right time. The Boston Celtics dynasty had ended, and everyone wondered which team would rise to the top that year. It turned out to be the Knicks, and they did it with a style of play that hadn't been seen in some time. In a way, the team was a throwback, playing the game as it was played in earlier times before players regularly soared above the rim and developed great one-on-one moves. With Eddie Donovan and Red Holzman constructing the kind of team they wanted, a team whose players not only had skills, but also the character to mesh those skills within the team concept, the Knicks caught the rest of the NBA by surprise. And when the league kind of caught up with their style, then the talent and character took over and carried them to the championship.

Take a look around the NBA today. The league is filled with great athletes who can handle the ball, soar above the rim, make great athletic moves, and amaze fans with a variety of slam dunks. But is there a team that plays the way the Knicks did, with five players blending together so they act like one? Not really. A few years ago I had occasion to speak with Willis Reed, who was writing a foreword for a *Basketball Almanac* I was writing. I remember saying to him at the time that I often speculated with several friends, all longtime followers of the game, about how the Knicks would fare against the teams and players of today. I told Willis we thought the 1969-1970 Knicks would more than hold their own in the modern NBA. He thought for a minute and then made a knowing kind of sound, an uh-huh that I interpreted as, *I wouldn't bet against us.*

I don't think anyone else would, either.

—Bill Gutman